## More Praise for Shari Hudspeth

"I have promoted from Senior Consultant to Director, Senior Director, and now Executive Director—all in one year! You are amazing and I thank you so much for your wisdom. My team knows that if Shari says to do it, DO IT!"
—*Lynn Pfost, Executive Director, Thirty-One Gifts*

"Shari is one of the best trainers in the industry. Her training helped me grow my business to new heights, including earning our company's incentive trip. Shari's excitement is contagious! The mentoring I received from Shari has been priceless and a major key to reaching my dreams. Thanks Shari!"
—*Jenifer Welch, Unit Leader, Simply Fun*

"Shari Hudspeth is simply the best motivator in the business. Her passion for the direct sales industry shines through. Her training took me from Unit Leader to Gold Director in sixteen months and tripled my income! She has years of experience in all areas of the direct sales world, and has a complete understanding of how the business works. If you are serious about your business, Shari can help you achieve all that you desire."
—*Sheri Quinn, Gold Director, Do-Re-Me & You!*

"Shari did a great job speaking and training at our conference. We were looking for easy, practical training to boost sponsoring. She really delivered great 'how-to' training that connected with our people. She did not come across as giving training that was developed 25 years ago. She was relevant to today's online, plugged-in, busy woman. We survey our conference attendees and she received the best ratings of any trainer we have used."
—*Mark Bosworth, CEO, SwissJust North America*

"I have had the pleasure of working extensively with Shari Hudspeth since she was chosen by my company to offer presentations and training to our sales field. The decision to hire Shari in this capacity has proven to be money well spent. As the founder of a direct sales company, I have found the combination of Shari's incredible success as a field leader and with her extensive experience in corporate positions to be the key element of her well-rounded and highly motivating presentations. Because of her multi-faceted background, Shari is able to effectively connect with a broad spectrum of audiences, from the newest representatives to rising stars and veteran leaders. From experience, I can say that Shari's programs, training and tools really work, and I recommend her with great confidence."
—*Rob Barnes, Founder, Sensaria Natural Bodycare*

"Thank you for bringing me back to the basics of my business. I learned the skills needed to book shows and grow my team. Your motivating words and your shared experiences have allowed me to maintain a full calendar while still enjoying free time with my family. Thank you for giving me the energy and direction to get my business fired up. You are an inspiration and a true leader."
—*Lisa Pevey, Consultant, PartyLite Gifts*

"Shari, I have said it before and I will say it again, you are truly amazing. Every piece of advice you have ever given, I have taken and I have used it. It has truly made a difference in my business. Thank you!"
—*Tabitha Ebbert, Senior Consultant, Thirty-One Gifts*

"Shari, you have truly inspired me to excel in my business! Your friendly, natural, transparent approach to people is refreshing and contagious. Thank you so much for not only offering the tools to help us excel, but also the training to go with it! It's an explosive combination!"
—*Christine Adams, Close To My Heart*

## About Shari Hudspeth and Average to Excellence

*Shari Hudspeth*
*Average to Excellence, LLC*
*(253) 630-2406*
*shari@averagetoexcellence.com*
*www.averagetoexcellence.com*

Shari has been actively involved in the direct sales industry since 1985, when she began her career as a field consultant. Her sales philosophy, tenacity and recruiting techniques hastened her ascent up the corporate ladder, earning her career-defining positions as corporate trainer and home office executive in several multi-million dollar organizations. As a result of working for various direct selling companies in high-level executive roles, her knowledge of the industry is vast and her experiences are diverse.

What sets Shari apart from other experts in the business is her first-hand experience in the field. Shari has personally built a fourteen million dollar annual sales team consisting of 140 leaders and six top-level leaders, all promoted through Shari. Even while managing a very robust downline, Shari still personally held 150 to 175 parties a year. Shari has since honed her formula and began teaching her methods, replicating her successes with other direct sellers and helping them build larger teams.

It's safe to say Shari is *the expert* when it comes to taking a direct selling business from average to excellence.

averagetoexcellence.com

# PARTY PLAN
# SUCCESS

## From Basics to
## BIG Results!

*Shari Hudspeth*

**THRIVE Publishing**
A Division of PowerDynamics Publishing, Inc.
San Francisco, California
**www.thrivebooks.com**

ISBN: 978-0-9836395-9-6

Library of Congress Control Number: 2011943504

Printed in the United States of America on acid-free paper.

URL Disclaimer

All Internet addresses provided in this book were valid at press time. However, due to
the dynamic nature of the Internet, some addresses may have changed or sites may have
changed or ceased to exist since publication. While the author and publisher regret any
inconvenience this may cause readers, no responsibility for any such changes can be accepted by either the author or the publisher.

This book is dedicated to all of my past and current personal coaching clients who have taught me so much. You are the reason my training is always cutting edge.

# TABLE OF CONTENTS

# ACKNOWLEDGEMENTS

Thank you to Ron Hudspeth, Reid Rohr, Carli Rohr and Brandon Bermudez— the amazing members of my executive team who keep me organized and put everything together perfectly! I couldn't do it all without you.

Thank you Tanya Branch, Barbie Collins Young, Cindy Carpenter, Lindsey Hale and Lynn Pfost for all your ideas and contributions. This book will be so much more helpful to direct sellers because you were willing to share your expertise.

Thank you to my many coaching clients over the years. You are what keeps me current and on the cutting edge. Because of you, if there is a shift in the market, I know about it!

Thank you to my daughter Jillian Leingang who inspires me every day and makes sure I stop and enjoy life frequently.

Most importantly, thank you to my parents Rene McAllister and Mary Ditch who modeled a strong work ethic for me my whole life. You taught me to work hard for what I want and to never give up. What greater gift can a parent give their child?

Finally to Derwin Ditch, my late stepfather, who from the day I stepped into direct sales was my biggest cheerleader, always believing in me and encouraging me to keep going when I wanted to quit. I miss you, Dad.

**Shari Hudspeth**

# INTRODUCTION

Welcome to *Party Plan Success*, the instruction manual for direct selling professionals. Whether you are a brand new consultant or a seasoned veteran in the field, you'll find everything you need to propel your business forward in today's market within these pages. Shari's extensive experience, coupled with constant interaction and feedback with her clients, sets her apart from other experts. She is continually evolving her training programs by actively addressing and solving the issues plaguing today's direct selling professional. Her incredibly positive influence on her coaching clients and their successfulness ensures you are getting the tips, terminology and techniques that work today—not a decade ago.

These chapters are your guide toward the fulfillment of your dreams. You'll find clear and simple step-by-step instructions for success: how to set goals, fill your calendar, build a team and everything in between.

This book is organized in three parts.
• Part One: Getting Your Business Off to a Fantastic Start
• Part Two: Business Basics for Big Results
• Part Three: Build Your Business Using Facebook

If you are just starting out, definitely start with the material in Part One. Then move on to Parts Two and Three. If you have been in the direct selling field for a while, you might find it useful to start with Part Two and move on to Part Three, although Part One will have some useful information and tools for you too.

Basically, what you have in your hands is a toolbox that you can use to expand and solidify your business, and enable you to achieve your dreams.

Your *Party Plan Success* toolbox includes:
- Templates for creating a contact list, setting goals and developing booking and recruiting seeds
- Scripts on how to book your first and subsequent parties, coach your hostesses and recruit friends and strangers
- How to use your calendar to maximize your business growth
- A clear explanation of what is happening in today's market and how to be successful in it
- How to set and achieve your goals
- The right phrases to get your hostesses to want to do what you ask
- A powerful checklist for effective hostess coaching
- How to recruit at your parties and easily leave with multiple bookings
- What to say (and what not to say) when talking to a booking or recruiting prospect
- How to handle objections graciously
- A sample customer information card that you can adapt for your business
- How to organize your office and manage your time to give you peace of mind

- The best way to use Facebook® to market your business and get bookings
- How to use Facebook to coach your hostesses, including instructions for setting up Facebook events
- Some critical do's and don'ts of Facebook and other social media

Please note that we have made a great effort to give you the most current terms and processes for using social media. However, as social media developers optimize their services for a continually changing digital culture, some of the terminology and ways of doing things may change over time.

Although everyone's definition of success is relative, we believe that anyone can achieve it with the help of this book. Some would be thrilled earning an extra $500 a month, while others dream of a six-figure income and the lifestyle it provides. Whatever your dreams of success are, with the right direction you can make them a reality. Shari is living proof that you don't need any special talents to have amazing success in this business. Remember this: success doesn't come from working really hard; it happens when you begin doing the right things.

If you are ready to get an awesome start in your new business or take your existing business to a new level, turn the page! Everything you need is right here.

*You are capable of excellence, so go for it!*

**—The Average To Excellence Team**

# PART ONE:

### Getting Your Business
### off to a

## FANTASTIC Start

# 1: GETTING STARTED THE EASY WAY

## You *Can* Do It!

You've made a great decision regarding getting involved in the direct sales industry! I believe it is the very best industry. The thing I like best about direct selling is that if you are highly educated, that's great. If you aren't, that's great too. I love that anybody can be hugely successful in this business.

Getting involved in direct sales in 1985 was one of the best decisions I ever made. I was one of those people who always struggled in school. I didn't go to college. In fact, I worked as a server and later a manager in a restaurant for 13 years. I went into childcare shortly after our second child was born so that I could be home and still earn an income. Please don't misunderstand me—I absolutely loved working at the restaurant and caring for children. I found both to be fun, rewarding and lucrative. However, those jobs would never have given me the opportunities that direct sales has!

## Unique Opportunities on Your Terms

In your new business, you will find opportunities for personal growth, friendships, prizes, recognition and income that I don't believe you can find anywhere else!

Where else could someone with a high school education, who was terrified to even introduce herself at her first meeting, earn a six-figure income? Where else can *you* decide you want to earn an extra $500 this month for school clothes or a mini vacation?

What other profession would give you prizes and, in some instances, even a free incentive trip to an exotic location just for doing your job? In this business, no one is trying to take your job or to outshine you. In fact, you'll find that your peers will help you succeed. They will share their fruitful ideas with you—and with each other—so that you are all successful! You will likely find that other consultants and leaders, and even many of your hostesses, will become some of your dearest friends. It's a great business. The best part is that it's your business. You get to decide what you want from your business, as well as how often and when you will work your business.

**Your Path To A Great Start**
Now let's talk about getting started the easy way! Whether you decide that you want to hold one party a week, or two or three or four in the future, I am absolutely convinced that there is only one way to get your business going the easy way . . . hold six parties in your first thirty days of business.

Why is this so important? It's important for many reasons. The biggest reason is this: most of us were nervous when it was time to do that first party. If you are like I was, that is an understatement! If we do one party every couple of weeks, we never get past that fear. It's like the first party every time. By doing several parties in a short period of time, we get past that wall. We begin to get a routine down, we get more comfortable with our presentation, and at each party we are a little more relaxed. As my husband is fond of saying, "Practice makes better!" Even after years and years in the business, I found that if I didn't do a party for a week, I was a little out of sync when I did the next one.

It's important to understand that if we are nervous, tense, and uncomfortable, so are our guests. Can you remember watching someone that was very nervous give a presentation? Do you remember how tense their nervousness made *you*? As we begin to relax and have fun at our parties, so do our guests. That's when you will see your sales and bookings increase!

## Fitting This into Life the Easy Way

After your six parties, you'll also have a better idea of how this is going to fit in your life. Many new consultants have told me that they thought that holding six parties in a month was going to completely overwhelm them, but they were surprised that it fit very nicely into their existing schedules. Some even said they felt they could hold more parties. I generally held three parties on Saturdays at 11:00 a.m., 3:00 p.m. and 7:00 p.m. Many of my new consultants followed that same schedule and loved the idea of holding three parties a week while only working one day.

## Implementing the "Fast and Furious" Start the Easy Way

Holding six parties in your first thirty days positively impacts your future income. On the other hand, holding only two parties will minimize your chance of success. Let's say in your first month you hold one party every couple of weeks and you book one new party from each of those two for the following month. In your second month, you might hold two parties if neither cancels. What if you get two bookings from those two for the next month? You *will* have a certain percentage of your bookings cancel, so ultimately you are on a path to hold only one to two parties per month and earn about $100 to $200 per month. This gives your business a weak start as well as a weak future.

Let's look at what getting a strong start by holding six parties in your first thirty days can do for you. You will earn about $600 in your first month. While you may only book one party from your first few, that will increase as you get more comfortable and relaxed. You will probably book eight to ten parties from your original six into your second month, and from those you could book twelve to fifteen into your third month. That could bring you $800 to $1,000 in income in your second month and $1,200 to $1,500 in your third month!

## Example - Weak Start

### Example - Weak Start

#### First Month of Business

1 show every 2 weeks
2 shows held x $300 sales = $600 sales
$600 sales x 30% commission = $180 income in first month
2 shows held x 1 booking per show = 2 scheduled shows for second month

#### Second Month of Business

2 shows x $300 sales = $600 sales
$600 sales x 30% commission = $180 income second month
2 shows x 1 booking = 2 scheduled shows for third month

#### Third Month of Business

1 show held (1 cancelled) x $300 sales = $90 income
300 in sales x 30% commission = $90 income for third month
1 show held x 1 booking = 1 show scheduled in fourth month

**Total income earned in first 3 months of business = $450.00**

## Example - Strong Start

### Example - Strong Start

#### First Month of Business

Six parties held in first month
Six parties x $350 in sales = $2,100 in sales
$2,100 in sales x 30% commission = $630 income
Six parties held x one booking from each of the first three parties held
Two bookings from each of the last three parties held = nine parties scheduled for second month,
(Bookings increase as you become more comfortable and more skilled)

#### Second Month of Business
Seven parties held second month, (two cancelled)
Seven parties x $375 in sales = $2,625 in sales,
(Your party average increases as your skills improve and you get more comfortable at your parties)
$2,625 in sales x 30% commission = $788.00 income
Seven parties held x two bookings per party = 14 parties scheduled into third month

#### Third Month of Business
11 parties held third month, (three cancelled) x $400 = $4,400 in sales
$4,400 in sales x 30% commission = $1,320 income
11 parties held x two bookings per party = 22 parties scheduled into fourth month

**Total income earned in first 3 months of business = $2,738.00**

I call this the fast and furious start versus the slow and painful start. "Fast and furious" is definitely more exciting! Decide now which approach you would like to take.

# 2: CREATING A GREAT CONTACT LIST

## Don't Pre-Judge

Now that you have clearly defined and written your goals, you are ready for the next step in getting your business off to a strong start: creating your contact list. This is the list of people you will be contacting to schedule your first parties. It is not unusual for a brand new consultant to book one party from every ten people contacted. Don't be discouraged! You're new. The more people you talk to, the better you will get, and soon you will schedule a party from one out of every five people you ask!

It is important to remember not to pre-judge the answer. If you don't ask someone if she would like to host a party, you really have decided for her that she wouldn't! People host parties for a number of reasons; to earn free product, to entertain, to be with friends, to show off their new furniture and so on. You never know why someone might say yes. Ask everyone and let each of them decide. Often, the person I was sure would say yes, said no, and the person I was sure would say no, said yes!

## Create Your Own F.R.A.N.K. List

As you begin to create the list of everyone you know, you may get stuck and find yourself unable to think of anyone else! That's where F.R.A.N.K. comes in. F.R.A.N.K. is an acronym for Friends, Relatives,

Acquaintances, Neighbors and Kid contacts. It's a way to jog your memory and remember people you might not easily recall.

- **Friends.** Think outside your best friends circle and expand it to any friends.
- **Relatives.** Think mom, sister, cousin, aunt, mother-in-law, sister-in-law, stepmom, brother, uncle and so on.
- **Acquaintances.** These are people like your hairdresser, manicurist and favorite grocery clerk, as well as coworkers, church acquaintances, or people you know from a group with which you are involved.
- **Neighbors.** This always reminds me of Anna. She came to an opportunity meeting I was holding in Idaho. She and her husband had just moved to Idaho that week. Her husband was in the military and had just been transferred. She didn't know a soul in town, but desperately wanted to get started in the business. She created a nice flyer and then went to each of her neighbors' homes on base and introduced herself. She explained she was new in town and was anxious to make new friends. She told them she was hosting a party that Tuesday and she would love it if they would come! Anna hosted her own party and had sixteen guests show up that night. We booked six parties from those guests—all because Anna stepped out of her comfort zone and spoke to complete strangers!
- **Kid contacts.** These are the parents in any groups you are involved with through your children: Boy Scouts, Girl Scouts, Brownies, Campfire Girls, soccer, baseball, hockey, Sunday school, PTA, play groups, MOPS and so on.

If you don't have your list of 100 when you have exhausted F.R.A.N.K., try mixing the categories up: your relatives' acquaintances, your friends' relatives and so on.

The other great thing about using F.R.A.N.K. is that you will have a very diverse list. I've seen consultants book their first parties all with family members or all with friends. The problem is that the same people are at all the parties! The first party is great, but then the sales drop and there are no more new bookings! By booking your first parties with different groups of people, you have a different crowd at each party, great sales and lots of bookings!

Your list of 100 is simply your starting point. From now on, keep the list with you. Whenever you think of someone new, you can add the name to the list. When you are out and about, meeting and sharing with new people, you can add those names to the list. That way your contact list is always growing.

# Creating A Contact List - Worksheet

## F.R.A.N.K.

F.riends
R.elatives
A.cquaintances
N.eighbors
K.ids contacts

| | | |
|---|---|---|
| 1 | 35 | 69 |
| 2 | 36 | 70 |
| 3 | 37 | 71 |
| 4 | 38 | 72 |
| 5 | 39 | 73 |
| 6 | 40 | 74 |
| 7 | 41 | 75 |
| 8 | 42 | 76 |
| 9 | 43 | 77 |
| 10 | 44 | 78 |
| 11 | 45 | 79 |
| 12 | 46 | 80 |
| 13 | 47 | 81 |
| 14 | 48 | 82 |
| 15 | 49 | 83 |
| 16 | 50 | 84 |
| 17 | 51 | 85 |
| 18 | 52 | 86 |
| 19 | 53 | 87 |
| 20 | 54 | 88 |
| 21 | 55 | 89 |
| 22 | 56 | 90 |
| 23 | 57 | 91 |
| 24 | 58 | 92 |
| 25 | 59 | 93 |
| 26 | 60 | 94 |
| 27 | 61 | 95 |
| 28 | 62 | 96 |
| 29 | 63 | 97 |
| 30 | 64 | 98 |
| 31 | 65 | 99 |
| 32 | 66 | 100 |
| 33 | 67 | |
| 34 | 68 | |

# 3: GETTING CONTROL OF YOUR CALENDAR

Early on I remember feeling completely out of control in my business. Some months I did a lot more parties than I wanted to do, while other months I wasn't doing enough parties to earn the money we were counting on. If somebody wanted to book a party on a Sunday, I'd grab it! I would always ask, "What day works best for you?" Then I would schedule whatever day she wanted at whatever time she wanted. If she wanted to schedule a party on my anniversary, I would think, "Well, that's the day she wants, and she's the customer so I should do it! After all, I don't want to lose this booking!"

As a result, I was completely out of control of my business, and often my personal life! Then I heard someone talk about calendar control and it literally changed my life.

Taking control of your calendar will ensure you are in control of your business!

The first step in taking control of your calendar is to pick your "party days." These are the days each week on which you will hold parties. They are the days that fit best in your personal schedule. For instance, for me, Sunday was a big family day and Friday was date night with my husband. I learned that I actually resented my business when

I agreed to do parties on these days. I felt I was missing out on something that I valued greatly.

My first step in getting control of my calendar was to choose Saturday and Tuesday as my party days. I could do three parties on Saturday at 11:00 a.m., 3:00 p.m. and 7:00 p.m., and one on Tuesday evening. My friend, who worked fulltime and wanted her weekends free, chose Monday, Tuesday and Wednesday, with one party on each of those evenings. She felt this worked well because it generally gave her four evenings and weekends to be with her family.

Keep in mind that doing three to four parties a week will likely generate a nice income for you. If you can only do one or two parties a week, then your income will be less.

### Here Are the Tools You Will Need

First, get yourself a calendar or a planner. This will be your one and only calendar. Everything you need to schedule, both personal and business, will go on this calendar. That way you won't schedule a time to call a hostess only to get home and find you have a doctor's appointment at that time. Next, you will need three highlighters in three different colors.

### Take These Two Simple Steps

The first thing you will want to do is take one of your highlighters (I used red for "heart") and mark off your family commitments that you absolutely do not want to miss for the next sixty days. Notice I said, "absolutely do not want to miss." Keep in mind that you are running your own business and that it will take some amount of sacrifice. You may miss some soccer practices or a piano lesson. However, you won't want to miss the state playoff or that big recital.

Next, take your second highlighter—perhaps a blue one—and mark off all meeting dates for the next sixty days. Meetings are usually once a month. You absolutely do not want to miss these. Although you might earn some money by holding a party that night, what you will learn at that meeting will continue to increase your income from the next party forward. Clearly, the bigger payoff comes from attending the meeting.

I rarely saw a consultant stay in the business if she didn't attend training meetings. There are two reasons to set aside the time for these events. You will learn new things, and more importantly, you will come away with a new, higher level of excitement and having built good relationships with your peers and the leader.

One more thing—even if you are brand new in the business, as soon as you know the dates of your national convention, mark those dates on your calendar. It is the once-a-year opportunity to hear from the best of the best in your company. The time and finances you invest in your convention will come back to you tenfold. Nearly every big success story I know started at a national convention.

Our convention always took place at the same time as our daughter Jillian's biggest horse show of the year. Although I desperately wanted to be there, I knew I needed to be at convention more. If I were to be as successful as I dreamed of being, I needed to hear how others were doing that, gleaning as much as I could from their experience and success and incorporating it into my business. It was hard to not be at my daughter's big event. However, both Jillian and I knew that without the income from my business, her having that beautiful horse would not have been possible.

Next, take your third highlighter (I suggest green for money) and highlight your party days, both those already scheduled and those that you need to fill. Looking at those empty green highlighted squares was a constant reminder of the days I still needed to fill to stay in control of my business.

## Two Important Benefits

One of the absolutely greatest things about having your calendar color-coded with available dates is that when someone wants to schedule a party, you can open up your calendar and they can see right away that this is a woman who takes her business seriously. It's also very easy to say, "The green squares are my party days, and I have Thursday the 7th at 7:00 p.m. or Saturday the 16th at 3:00 p.m. Which one works better for you?" The next thing you know, she picks one and you've just booked a party!

The really great thing about taking control of your calendar is that when people see that you take your business seriously, so do they. They see that you are a professional. When I started doing this, my cancellation rate dropped drastically. They respected me. They could see how limited my availability was and knew that if they cancelled, it might be a while before they could get another date.

## Time to Take Action

If you already have a calendar that you use, that's great. Otherwise, make it a priority to get the tools you need right away. If you prefer an electronic version that works on your computer and your smart phone or iPad®, make sure the two devices sync automatically, and select three different colors to use—to represent the highlighters you would use on a paper calendar. Just as you would show your paper calendar to a potential hostess, you can show her your calendar on your phone or iPad.

Get control of your calendar, and you will not only get control of your business, you will find that you have control of your life, resulting in less stress and more ease! For more tips on how to keep your sanity and maximize your results, see the chapter on prioritizing that starts on page 143 at the end of Part Two.

| Sample Month at-a-glance | | | October | | | |
|---|---|---|---|---|---|---|
| Sun | Mon | Tue | Wed | Thu | Fri | Sat |
| | | | 1 | 2 Date w/hubby | 3 11a-Barbara 3p-Susie 7p-Nikki | |
| 4 Family day | 5 6:30p-Liz | 6 6:30p (Still need to book) | 7 | 8 | 9 Date w/hubby | 10 |
| 11 Family day | 12 7p-Unit Meeting | 13 | 14 | 15 | 16 Date w/hubby | 17 11a-Jenny 3p-Alexa 7p-Melissa |
| 18 Family day | 19 | 20 | 21 | 22 | 23 Date w/hubby | 24 |
| 25 Family day | 26 6:30p-Jill | 27 6:30p-Mandy | 28 | 29 | 30 Date w/hubby | 31 |

# 4: BOOKING YOUR FIRST SIX PARTIES

There are two critical mistakes a new consultant often makes. The first mistake is that she creates what I call her "A" list from her friends and family whom she is sure will help her start her new business by booking a party. When the consultant starts calling her "A" list and gets a few no's, she gets discouraged. She often thinks, "If my friends and family won't book a party, then nobody will!" New consultants sometimes give up before they even get started! The truth is that our friends and family are some of the hardest people to book! They don't always take our new business as seriously as strangers do. The other piece is that they often have not seen the product yet and simply aren't as excited as a guest at a party who has just experienced a presentation might be. That's why you want to make sure you have an extensive list of people to contact so that even when you get some no's, you still have many other people to contact to get your yes's.

The second mistake is not being persistent (giving up). Keep calling and you will get your yes's!

### Offer Fun—Don't Ask For a Favor

It has been a long time since I was a brand new consultant. However, I seem to remember the things I did wrong all too well. I can remember that my perception was that I needed to get my friends and family to do a favor for me and help me get my business started. I can even remember who my first hostesses were!

I called everyone I could think of and told them I was going to sell educational toys, and asked if they would help me get my business going. Of course my mom said yes. She wasn't excited, but she said yes anyway. My sister did not like hosting or attending parties and said, "Please don't make me do this", but eventually she said yes. My friend Kristi, who would do just about anything for me, said yes, and my friend Debbie agreed to host. There were many, many more who said no!

My mom called a few friends and told them her daughter had gotten involved in some toy company and she had to have a party for her, and that if they weren't doing anything that night, she was making an apple cake and they were welcome to come! Her party had three people and the sales were $120 and zero bookings. My sister had her party at her office. She told her coworkers that her sister was making her have a toy party and asked them to please come so it wouldn't be a total flop! Her party was worse! Kristi had fifteen guests, $800 in sales and eight bookings! Debbie had eight guests. Her sales were $500 and I got five bookings!

I did have some success from my first parties, but it wasn't my fault! Kristi and Debbie were just really committed to helping me. I didn't know it at the time, but I had made a critical mistake in booking those first parties. What's worse is that I continued to make the same mistake for some time. Remember, I said that my perception was that I needed to ask a favor. Doing that implies that there is nothing in it for the other person except to have a warm fuzzy feeling for helping someone out.

If you feel like you are asking for a favor—and you don't like to do that—it will come through in your voice. On the other hand, if you think you are offering to help or you are making a fun offer, it will sound entirely different. I didn't realize then that I really did have something great to offer. It is easier to offer than to ask, and people get excited about W.I.I.F.M., which stands for "what's in it for me."

Do you think my mom might have been more excited if I told her that she could get some really great, award-winning toys for her grandchildren to play with at her house for free? Would my sister have been more excited if I had told her that many of the toys we offered had won national awards, that her daughter Melissa loved the puzzle that I had bought, that it was also a tracing game, that you could use the shapes to cut out play dough or cheese or bologna and that you could make rub-ons with it?

What if I had told her that she could get that puzzle and several other great games and toys for free? My hostesses were completely in the dark. I hadn't given them any idea of what we offered or what they could get by hosting a party. I'm sure they would have invited people with much more enthusiasm and conviction if I had shared that information with them. I'm sure my mom and sister's parties would have had much different results.

When you begin to call people to book your first parties, you'll want to focus on what's in it for your friend or family member. Think about what would get them excited about hosting a party! If your company doesn't already have a script for you to use, see the sample booking script at the end of this chapter.

### Set Yourself a Short Deadline

Most direct selling companies have incentives for moving quickly when you first start your business. If your company has such an incentive, do go for it. It will make a huge difference in the success of your business.

No matter what, consider getting those first six parties booked quickly. Give yourself a one-week deadline to book the parties, and schedule them during the first thirty days of your business. You will be amazed at the momentum that you will have as you focus on reaching this goal. See the chapter on goal setting on page 45 for a great system to use for setting this goal and for breaking it down into manageable steps.

## Final Thoughts

Keep these two things in mind as you book your first six parties: Focus on what's in it for your potential hostesses and be persistent. If one person says no, go on to the next. You could even ask the person who said no who she knows that might be interested in getting some free product in exchange for inviting a few people over. You never know—maybe that no will turn into a yes.

Start now and make that plan for how you will book your first six parties. You will be glad you did!

# Sample - Short Script
### (Should take less than 10 minutes)

## Introduction:
**Shari:** Hi Jill, its Shari.

**Jill:** Oh, Hi Shari! It's great to hear from you!

## Permission:
**Shari:** Thanks Jill! It's great to talk with you too! I know it's close to dinner time, but I wonder if I could chat with you for a few minutes?

**Jill:** Sure. I have just a few minutes. Then I have to start dinner.

## Purpose:
**Shari:** I promise to be brief, but I wanted to tell you about something that I think you will love!

**Jill:** Sure, go ahead!

## Benefit:
**Shari:** Well, I'm so excited! I just signed up to be a consultant with this amazing candle company. We offer about 50 different scents, an assortment of traditional and unique candles and some really beautiful accessories to go with them! I know how much you love candles, so you were the first person I called. I'm booking my first parties to get started. Of course you'd be helping me, but if you'd like to host a party, you'll earn some really beautiful products for free! And, with all your friends, I bet you'd get quite a bit for free! There is one piece that I think you would really love! It's a large table stand that would be perfect in your living room!

## Objection: (feel, felt, found)
**Jill:** Wow! You sound really excited! I do love candles, especially when they're free, and I'd really love to help you get started. But, honestly Shari, I am so busy, I just don't think I have time!

**Shari:** I can certainly understand that! Life gets busier and busier! I know I really didn't have time to go to Mary's candle party the other night, but, you know what, after I was there for a little while, I couldn't believe how relaxed I felt! I realized it had been a long time since I had done something just for me. Being with my girlfriends was just what I needed! It might be nice for you to have some time with your friends AND, get some free product. What do you think?

**Jill:** That's true. We haven't gotten together for awhile.

## Close:
**Shari:** Would you like to go ahead and schedule a party with your friends? I just know you'll have a great time.

**Jill:** Okay, sure.

**Shari:** Great! I have Thursday the 28th and Tuesday the 19th, which one works best for you?

**Jill:** Tuesday the 19th works best.

**Shari:** Okay, I've got you down for Tuesday the 19th. I'm going to send you a hostess packet. I'll follow-up in a couple of days to make sure you received it. In the meantime, go ahead and start creating your guest list. Your friends, of course, but don't forget family and coworkers!

# 5: GETTING THE MOST FROM YOUR FIRST SIX PARTIES

You've worked hard to book your first six parties! You want to make sure the scheduled parties occur and that you get the most from them. One of the best ways to ensure that happening is by doing a good job of hostess coaching.

There is an extensive chapter on hostess coaching in Part Two of this book. This chapter will focus on coaching your first six hostesses, who are likely to be friends and family. We discussed in the previous chapter, "Booking Your First Six Parties," how friends and family can sometimes be the toughest to book. Friends and family may not take your business seriously and they most likely have not been to a party to see how much fun it is and how great your product is. That's why it is very important to do a great job of coaching these hostesses and really helping them to have fantastic parties. These parties are the launching pad for the future of your business!

## Important First Goal

You'll want to end up with at least eight to ten bookings from your first six parties. Let me explain why. Imagine you book one party from each party. You held six and you have six booked into the next month. There will be a certain number of cancellations. A typical cancellation rate is 25 percent. If you have six parties booked into month two, you will probably hold five. If you book one party from each of those, you will have five booked into month three. With cancellations, you will hold four. Can you see where this pattern is taking you?

It is easier to get multiple bookings from your first six parties when you have eight or more guests in attendance than when you have three or four. Your hostesses don't know how to have a great party with great attendance. They need your help!

### Ten Things You Can Do to Help Your Hostess Have a Great Party

**1. As soon as your hostess commits to a date, send her a handwritten thank you card.** This is a lost art. No one does this anymore, so when someone receives a handwritten note, it is very special and it makes that person feel much appreciated. Even though you did a great job of sharing what she will get for hosting a party, a big part of the reason she is having a party is because she is your friend or family member and she wants to help you. Helping a friend is the number three reason people book parties today.

**2. Ask her how she would like to invite her guests.** Would she prefer to invite them by phone, email, text or Facebook®? Maybe she would like to do a little of each. If she prefers Facebook, set up her event for her as explained in Part Two in the chapter, "Coaching Your Hostess Using Facebook" starting on page 167.

**3. Help her create a guest list.** Give her ideas of who to invite. Make sure she has at least forty names on her list. Thirty to fifty percent will attend. This will give you great attendance at your first parties, which will help make the parties lively and fun! Fun parties equal great sales and lots of bookings!

**4. Tell her what to say when inviting her guests.** If you don't coach the new hostess, the invitation will likely sound something like this: "My daughter just signed up to be a _____consultant and I'm having her first party. Can you come?" Instead, coach her to say something like this: "My daughter just signed up with ____. Their product line is right up your alley! You're going to love it. Besides, when's the last time you had a night off with girlfriends? You need a break! Can I put you down as a yes?"

**5. Thank her on every contact.** The more appreciated she feels, the less likely she is to cancel and the harder she will work to make sure she has a successful party.

**6. Stay in close contact with her.** Remind her how much fun it is going to be and what a nice break it will be for her and her friends.

**7. Encourage her to keep the snacks simple.** The more elaborate the food, the fewer bookings you will get. While the guests love the wonderful food and it can increase attendance, most guests will not want to make that kind of effort or financial investment. Consequently, they don't book parties themselves. The easier hosting a party looks, the more bookings you will get.

**8. Encourage theme parties.** Attendance is higher at theme parties. It adds an extra element of fun for the guests. Here are just a few theme ideas:

- Pajama party (guests wear their pajamas). It is actually a very popular theme party.
- Mexican fiesta (nachos or tacos with Mexican decorations)
- Funny slipper contest
- Crazy flip-flop contest
- Death by chocolate party
- Chicks and chocolate
- Halloween costume contest

**9. If her party is a Facebook event, be sure you are jumping in often and posting comments** like "Aunt Mary, I'm so glad you're coming, you always make everything more fun!" "Joanne, you are going to love this line!" "Jennifer, look at all the people coming to your party! This is going to be 'The Party' to be at. All the cool people are going to be there!" You can also comment on other people's posts to start building rapport before the party even starts. Check in often to see if there are questions you can answer as well.

**10. The day before her party have your hostess connect with her guests to remind them.** If she does this she will have three more guests attend for every twenty she invited. People are so busy today that they need that last reminder or they will forget. She will more than likely be hesitant to do this. You will hear "I already invited them and sent and Evite® or postcard. I don't want them to think I am pushing them into something they don't want to do." You can respond with this: "I completely understand, I wouldn't want my friends to think I was trying to push them into something either. The challenge is that they want to attend, they just have such busy lives they forget and then are disappointed the next day when they find out they missed out on a really fun evening. What if you say, 'Hi, Jill, I am getting ready to make my snacks for tomorrow night and I want to have enough. Were you planning on bringing your sister with you?' This way it just feels like you want to be prepared, you actually reminded them to attend and said that they could bring a friend! Does that feel more comfortable?"

Taking the time to coach your first six hostesses this way will ensure that you have great sales and lots of bookings from your first parties. This is the way to get your business off to a fantastic start!

# 6: RECRUIT A FRIEND

What is the most exciting thing you can do for your new business? Recruit a friend!

Are you nervous about attending meetings where the only person you know is the person who recruited you? Recruit a friend! She will go with you.

Do you wish you had somebody to talk to about your new business? Someone who is as excited as you are? Somebody who is experiencing the same fears you are? Recruit a friend! You can encourage each other, you can tell each other how wonderful you are and you can celebrate each other's successes.

Who will be the proudest person in the room when you get recognized at a meeting? Your friend! It is so much fun to do this business with a friend!

## How Do I Do That?
1. If you joined because you wanted to earn an extra $400 a month, you're probably already thinking of a friend that you know needs extra money. That's great, although she is not the only person to call for one very important reason. She might say no. When you were booking your first parties, some people you called said yes and

possibly many said no. What if you had only called six people? You probably wouldn't have gotten six parties. Statistically, if you ask ten people to join you, one will. Therefore, you want to ask ten friends to do this business with you.

2. Think about your friends who might join for the same reason you did, and people who might be interested for a different reason. People join this business for many reasons and your friend might be very excited about something you didn't even think about when you joined. She might be very excited about earning a free trip to an exotic location. Maybe some of your friends have young children or teenagers and the thought of getting out to do a party one night a week and get some "me" time is very appealing! Maybe your friend is the competitive sort and likes the idea of being a top seller or recruiter. She might crave recognition and would love to be recognized at meetings. It could be that she loves being center stage, standing in front of a group and having all the attention on her for thirty minutes. You never know what someone's hot button might be.

3. When you were getting ready to make your booking calls, you were thinking about what would excite the person you were contacting. Now think about how the business opportunity could benefit your friend or family member. You have a much better chance of getting a yes if you are speaking to their needs and desires. Use the worksheet in this chapter to help you. If you aren't able to fill it out completely, that's okay. As you think of people, continue to fill it out as those additional names come to mind. Now you have a better idea of why each of your friends or family members might join.

4. What do you say when you call? The initial call is to generate interest. You just want to get her thinking and excited about the possibility. As in booking calls, you can easily give too much information. When a prospective recruit gets overwhelmed and doesn't understand everything you said, she will just say no. You want to focus on the

one thing you know will interest her. There are sample scripts in this chapter for many different needs and desires, as well as for handling some of the objections you might get.

As with your booking calls, when you focus on the other person, it's a much easier, more comfortable conversation. You will also find that you get better results when you talk about why this might be a good fit for that particular person. Look over Sample Script #1 in this chapter. We'll cover how to follow up with your prospects shortly.

## What Goes in the Recruiting Packet

I've seen consultants give out recruiting packets that had so much information in them they weighed about five pounds. There were catalogs, handmade flyers, recruiting brochures, income charts, hostess brochures, new consultant checklists, training on how to get started, how to earn the trip in your first three months, the company mission statement, meeting dates for the next year . . . talk about overwhelming! A prospect receiving that kind of packet would take a look at all that information and within three minutes say, "This is too hard! There's too much to learn." This is a simple business and we need to present it simply. All you need in your packet is a catalog, your company's recruiting brochure, and if there is a recruiting promotion going on—a "sign up this month and get this offer"— then a copy of the promotion. That's it! Remember, at this point you are trying to generate interest, not train your prospects

Paper doesn't recruit people—people recruit people. The packet will provide some details and some food for thought. However, it's your excitement about what you're doing, you sharing what would be great for them, and your belief that they could do this that will ultimately recruit them.

## The Most Important Step

You've called your friend, you've shared your excitement about the business, you've told her why she might really enjoy being a consultant and you've given her some information to look over. What's the next step? I hope you're not thinking, "If she decides to join, she'll call me. She's my friend, I don't want to pressure her", because she won't! You have to call her. Your friend is busy, has three young children, and is distracted and tired. She has thought about it off and on, and by the time she gets to the end of her day she can't even think.

Call your prospect. Call within 24 hours of when you gave her the information, while it is fresh in her mind and while there is still interest.

## Here's How to Follow Up

Here's an example of the short script to use for this step. Note that Kathy is looking for a social outlet.

**You:** Hi Kathy, it's Shari. Is this a good time to talk? Good! Have you given any more thought to getting out of the house once a week? (Remind her of what appealed to her.) You have? Great! You have some questions? Okay, I'll answer whatever I can and if I don't know the answer, I'll call my leader and get it for you! (You'll be surprised at how simple the questions are, and you probably asked your upline the same questions, so you'll know most of the answers.) How much does it cost to get started? Well, the kit is blah blah and you will probably earn that back at your first party! (Resist the temptation to tell her everything she gets in her kit. That's too much information for this stage.)

**Kathy:** Do I have to go to meetings?

**You:** Are you kidding? That's going to be one of your favorite parts. They are so much fun, and you'll get ideas to make your parties more fun, too. (Remember she is looking at this opportunity as a social outlet. Focus on that.) You'll give it a try? Yeah! I'm so glad. We're going to have so much fun doing this together. What I am going to do now is have my upline call you and she'll tell you what you need to do to get started. It's really simple. What time is a good time for her to call you today? Between three and four? Okay, I'll have her call you. Please call me after you talk with her. Bye, Kathy.

It is important to get her signed up right away. It's human nature to have self-doubt, so have your upline call her while she is excited, before she has time to question her decision. Your friend will soon thank you for sharing something with her that was just what she needed.

# Recruit A Friend Contact List

List the names of friends and family under the category you think might interest them:

| Fun | Get out of the house | Recognition |
|---|---|---|
| 1. | 1. | 1. |
| 2. | 2. | 2. |
| 3. | 3. | 3. |
| 4. | 4. | 4. |
| 5. | 5. | 5. |

| Center of Attention | Competitive | Part of a fun group |
|---|---|---|
| 1. | 1. | 1. |
| 2. | 2. | 2. |
| 3. | 3. | 3. |
| 4. | 4. | 4. |
| 5. | 5. | 5. |

| Loves the product | Social | Likes to help people |
|---|---|---|
| 1. | 1. | 1. |
| 2. | 2. | 2. |
| 3. | 3. | 3. |
| 4. | 4. | 4. |
| 5. | 5. | 5. |

| Flexibility | Earn Money | Free Trip |
|---|---|---|
| 1. | 1. | 1. |
| 2. | 2. | 2. |
| 3. | 3. | 3. |
| 4. | 4. | 4. |
| 5. | 5. | 5. |

| Free Product and Prizes | | |
|---|---|---|
| 1. | 1. | 1. |
| 2. | 2. | 2. |
| 3. | 3. | 3. |
| 4. | 4. | 4. |
| 5. | 5. | 5. |

# Example - Short Script 1

**Sample Script**

<u>Interest</u>: Get out of the house and have some "*me*" time.

**Introduction:**

**Shari:** Hi Kathy! It's Shari!

**Kathy:** Oh hi, how are you?

**Shari:** I'm great! How are you?

**Kathy:** I'm good, what's up?

**Permission:**

**Shari:** Well, I want to talk to you about something I think might be really exciting for you. Do you have just a few minutes?

**Kathy:** Sure!

**Purpose:**

**Shari:** Well, you know I just joined XYZ Company, right?

**Kathy:** Yes! I know you're really excited about making some extra money.

**Shari:** I'm actually really excited! I've got my parties booked, and that was easier than I thought, and I really think it's going to help our financial situation. But, I'm calling you because I was thinking about you today and how much you love going to parties like this! It's your little break; your downtime!

**Kathy:** Oh, I look forward to those breaks! In fact, Adam just colored his bedroom wall today with his crayons! Today would be an excellent day for a break!

**Benefit:**

**Shari:** Oh no! What if you could go to a party once a week? If you joined XYZ Company you could get out of the house and have some "Kathy time" every week!

**Kathy:** You mean sell?

**Shari:** Yes! You'd be great! Everybody loves you!

**Objection:** (Feel, felt, found)

**Kathy:** Oh I don't know, I don't think I could stand up and talk in front of people.

**Shari:** I know, I'm nervous about that too, but my leader said that's normal. She felt that way at the beginning too, but by the time she did a few parties she felt more relaxed. She realized people were paying more attention to the product and each other than her! She said I could sit on the floor or in a chair if I wanted to; if it would make me more comfortable.

**Kathy:** That's true. I do go to those parties more to visit than anything else, and I never thought about sitting down.

**Close:**

**Shari:** Kathy, you really don't have anything to lose. You can try it for a few weeks. If you don't like it you can quit, but it may be just what you need! You don't need to decide today. Why don't I bring a little information by. You can talk to John about it and I'll call you tomorrow and see if you have any questions. How does that sound?

**Kathy:** Okay, that sounds fine.

**Shari:** Great! I'll see you later today.

# Example - Short Script 2

<u>Sample Script</u>

## <u>Interest:</u> Money

**Introduction:**
   **Shari:** Hi Barbie, its Shari
   **Barbie:** Oh, Hi Shari! What's up!

**Permission:**
   **Shari:** I wondering if I could chat with you for a few minutes?
   **Barbie:** Okay, sure.

**Purpose:**
   **Shari:** I want to tell you about something I think you'll be interested in.

**Benefit:**
   **Shari:** You know I just joined XYZ company, right?
   **Barbie:** Yes! I know you're really excited about making some extra money.

   **Shari:** I'm actually really excited! I've got my parties booked  and that was easier than I thought, and I think it's really going to help our financial situation, but the reason I'm calling you is I've been thinking about you a lot lately. You mentioned that you're thinking about looking for a job. Barbie, why don't you think about becoming a consultant? If you just hold two parties a week, you could earn about $800 a month. You could work around your schedule instead of someone telling you when to work. Would $800 a month take off some of the stress?

**Objection:** (Feel, felt, found)
   **Barbie:** Oh sure! But, I think I need something steady, where I know I have a certain income each month.
   **Shari:** I can understand that Barbie. I was worried about that too, but the more I thought about it, I remembered all the people I know who have been laid off lately. This would be your business and no one could lay you off. Even if you took a job, how many hours would you have to work to earn $800? You'd only be working about 6 hours a week as a consultant to earn that!
   **Barbie:** Really?

**Close:**
   **Shari:** Really! Why not try it for a few weeks and see what you think?
   **Barbie:** Okay, I'll try it and see how it goes.

# Example - Short Script 3

**Sample Script**

<u>Interest:</u> Fun

**Introduction:**
Shari: Hi, Liz, its Shari!
Liz: Hi Shari!

**Permission:**
Shari: Do you have a few minutes?
Liz: Sure, I have a few minutes.

**Purpose:**
Shari: I have something to share with you that I think you'll love!

**Benefit:**
Shari: I just signed up to be a consultant with XYZ company. I went to a meeting on Monday and had a blast, and then I went to a party with my up line and watched her do a presentation! It was so much fun to be at the party and see how excited everyone was about the product, and to see how much fun everyone was having! It made me think of you, and how much you like to have fun! I think this is something you would love to do yourself! We could go to meetings together! It would be so much fun to do this with you! What do you think?

**Objection:** (Feel, felt, found)
Liz: Oh Shari, you know how I hate to pressure people. I don't think this is something I'd enjoy very much.
Shari: I can totally relate to that! I was worried about that too, but we needed the money, so I decided to try it. What I've learned is that the guests come to the party expecting to buy something. They are really excited about what they order and have a great time with friends! Think about when you go to the mall to buy a new outfit. You go expecting to buy something. You have fun shopping, especially if you go with a friend, and you leave excited about your new outfit!
Liz: That's a good point!

**Close:**
Shari: Why don't you try it for a few weeks and see what you think?
Liz: What if I don't like it?
Shari: I'd be really surprised if you don't love it! The worst thing that can happen is that you tried it, made some fun money, and got some great product in your kit! I think you'd be great!
Liz: Okay, I'll try it!

## Example - Short Script 4

<u>**Sample Script**</u>

<u>Interest</u>: Loves the product

<u>**Introduction:**</u>
    **Shari:** Hi Mary! It's Shari!
    **Mary:** Oh Hi Shari, how are you?
    **Shari:** Pretty excited these days!

<u>**Permission:**</u>
    **Shari:** Do you have a few minutes?
    **Mary:** Just a few, I have to get Carli to swim practice.
    **Shari:** No problem! This will just take a few minutes.

<u>**Purpose:**</u>
    **Shari:** I've been thinking about you and I wanted to talk to you about something.
    **Mary:** Okay, what's up?

<u>**Benefit:**</u>
    **Shari:** I know you have a party scheduled with me next week, but I didn't want to wait that long! I've been thinking about how much you love XYZ product! Every time we go to a party you are telling everyone about all the cool things this product does or why they just have to buy that product! You are selling the product at every party you go to. Why not sign up, become a consultant, and get paid for it?

<u>**Objection:**</u> (Feel, felt, found)
    **Mary:** Oh no! I'm so busy already. There's no way I could take something else on.
    **Shari:** You are busy Mary! I almost didn't call you because I know how busy you are! But then I thought, "Mary goes to all the parties anyway," why not call her and see if she'd like to make money at the parties instead of spend it?
    **Mary:** Good point!

<u>**Close:**</u>
    **Shari:** Why not try it for a few weeks and see how it feels? If it's too much, you can stop, but as much as you love the product and love to talk about it, I think you'll be great and I think you'll have a lot of fun!
    **Mary:** Okay, I'll try it for a few weeks and see how it feels.

# 7: PREPARING FOR YOUR FIRST PARTY

## Collecting Your Supplies

The more organized and prepared you feel going into your first party, the less nervous you will be! Doing these few simple steps will help you feel organized and prepared. Here are some things you will need to get started:

- Folders
- Ink pens
- A rubber stamp with your name, address, phone number and email or labels for marking catalogs, envelope and brochures (The nice thing about labels is that they don't smear.)
- Fabric if you plan on using fabric for your display
- A money bag
- Change for your money bag
- 8½" by 11" envelopes for hostess packets and recruiting packets
- Raffle tickets (for games)
- Simple inexpensive prizes for games (I often used candy bars. Chocolate is always a hit!)
- A cloth tote bag or briefcase to carry your guest folders, hostess packets, recruiting packets, money bag and pens to your party
- A second tote bag or rolling bag (depending on how large your product is) to carry your product to your parties

**Feeling Organized and Prepared for any Party**

First, stamp or label all of your materials, envelopes and guest copies of the guest order form. You want your guest to know how to contact you in case she has a problem with an order or wants to place future orders.

Next, put together guest folders. I always gave a folder to each guest at my parties. It looks professional, it is inexpensive, and it gives the customer something on which to write. I collected the extras at the end of each party. Make thirty to forty guest folders ahead of time. Take fifteen guest folders to each party so you'll be sure to have enough. Put a catalog, guest order form, hostess brochure and recruiting brochure in each folder. That way the guests can be looking over the product, hostess opportunity and recruiting opportunity while they are waiting for the party to get started.

Some consultants feel that giving out the catalog at the beginning of the party, before they have a chance to talk about the product, will hurt their sales or tempt the customers to flip through the catalog and not pay attention to the presentation. I felt the same way until I asked one of my top sellers what she did to get such high sales. Surprisingly, she told me that she gave out the catalog at the beginning of the party. So I decided to try it. Changing that one thing raised my party average $100! She said, "Who cares if they flip through the catalog while I'm talking? If my party is fun and interactive, they are listening!" She was right!

In addition to guest folders, make fifteen to twenty hostess packets ahead of time. Take six hostess packets to each party. Include two catalogs, eight guest order forms, one hostess brochure, one recruiting brochure and one copy of any hostess or customer specials in each hostess packet.

Finally, put together ten recruiting packets. Take three recruiting packets to each party. Include a catalog, a recruiting brochure and a copy of any promotions or incentives for joining the business that month in each recruiting packet.

Now that you have all your packets ready, pack your tote bag with fifteen guest folders, six hostess packets, three recruiting packets and your money bag with change and pens.

Practice setting up your product display and putting it away a couple of times before your party. The practice will give you two benefits: you can see how you want everything to look before you get to your first party and you can master a quick set-up and take-down.

## Learn from Experienced Leaders

Go to one or two of your upline leader's parties to observe. You can learn a lot from just watching someone else. Don't interrupt her party with questions or comments. Just listen. Even though I had been doing parties for years and years, I would ask to observe someone who was having great success at one of her parties. I learned a great deal watching successful people in action!

Once you've observed one or two parties, practice your party at least two times. Practice out loud, just like it is the real thing. You'll feel much more comfortable at your first party if it's not the first time you do it out loud. To this day, whenever I am going to give a presentation I go through it out loud several times. It flows much better when I do it live!

## Ready to Go!

Pack your product and load your car! You're ready *and* prepared to host your first party!

# PART TWO:

## Business Basics for

# BIG Results

# 8: HOW TO GET GREAT RESULTS THROUGH EFFECTIVE GOAL SETTING

Of all the business-building skills we can acquire, goal setting is the most important. It's the difference between taking what you get and getting what you want! Without a clear goal in mind, anything will do.

Elizabeth, one of my consultants, had returned from our national convention. The president had given a challenge to all the consultants attending to go home and book fourteen parties in 48 hours! That's a pretty big goal. Elizabeth was committed to making this year different from her past years in the business. She accepted the challenge and went to work making booking calls. She didn't hit fourteen, but she did book twelve parties in 48 hours!

There's a great quote from motivational speaker, speech coach and bestselling author Les Brown that says: "Shoot for the moon. Even if you miss, you'll land among the stars!" How many parties do you think Elizabeth would have booked without that clear goal? Would she even have gotten on the phone in her first 48 hours at home?

Elizabeth had her best month to date as a result of booking those twelve new parties. Her sales were over $5,000! Although she did not hit her exact goal of booking fourteen parties in 48 hours, she had the best sales month in her career! Remember that ordinary people achieve extraordinary things as the result of goal setting.

### The Rewards of Goal Setting: An Example from Our Family

When our children were young, we had a rule at our house: If you wanted something extra, you had to earn it. They could do chores around the house, label my catalogs, put hostess packets together, fold clothes and so on. We wanted to instill a solid work ethic in our children.

When our son was twelve, there was a computer game he wanted that required more memory than we currently had. Reid decided to pick blueberries that summer to earn the necessary money for the computer memory chip. Now, think about blueberries—they are very small and the pay was only 25 cents a pound. Can you imagine how many blueberries it takes to fill a five-pound bucket and what that is worth? $1.25! On his first day he picked forty pounds and earned $10. He had been picking around bees and spiders all day in the heat, and was dirty, tired and grumpy. He grumbled all the way home about how hard it was and how his older sister was earning $20 a day babysitting.

I complained to my husband that night that the thirty-minute drive each way in a gas-guzzling Suburban to drop him off and pick him up was costing us more than he was making, in addition to the two hours driving time each day. Ron was adamant that this was a good experience for Reid and that quitting was not a quality we wanted to instill in our children. Consequently, every day we made the trek to the blueberry field, and every day Reid picked thirty to forty pounds, grumbling all the way home. I silently grumbled with him! Each day we tried to inspire him to pick more and he would tell us he was working as hard as he could.

Then something happened at the end of the first week. Reid got paid! There is something about a twelve-year-old boy having $35 cash in his hand. It really motivated him. On Monday he said, "I think I'll try to pick fifty pounds today!" He picked 53. On Tuesday he was more definite, stating, "Today, I'm going to pick sixty!" He didn't really understand it, but he was setting goals and his reaction to achieving them was very typical.

Wednesday, he said in a more confident voice, "Today, I'm going to pick 68." He skipped his breaks and took a short lunch because he wanted to hit his goal. He picked 74 pounds!

It became a game each night to guess how much he had picked that day. I can still see the huge smile on Reid's face as we tried to guess. Before that summer, in spite of our constant praise, Reid struggled with low self-esteem and was a mediocre student, though when he was young we had been told he was gifted.

That summer we could see his self-esteem and confidence growing each day. On Friday, if he'd had a personal best that week, we took him out for ice cream. Between gas, ice cream and time this was proving to be an expensive summer. However, what I learned that summer is that you can't put a price on self-esteem or self-confidence. It would have been a big mistake to let him quit that first week.

Reid's goals kept growing. Now, not only was he skipping breaks and taking shorter lunches, he was calling to tell us to pick him up an hour later so he could pick even more!

One evening, Clarissa, the owner of the fields, came over to the car as Reid was getting in. She said, "Your son is the hardest worker I've ever had. You should be really proud of him." Ahhh . . . recognition! Talk about motivation. He worked even harder, he broke the existing records and then he broke his own! He got prizes for breaking the record every week. On his best day that summer he picked 124 pounds of very small blueberries. Clarissa made him the lead picker and put him in charge of the other workers, training the new kids.

As the season came to a close, the berries were fewer and fewer. On the last day Ron said "if you pick forty pounds today, I'll buy you that video game you want." Of course Dad is thinking the berries are slim pickings now, and it's going to be tough to reach forty pounds. However, of course Reid did it anyway. Reid got his memory for the computer, a CD player and the video game. However, that summer he got so much more. That summer at the blueberry fields changed Reid's life, and the next school year he got straight A's. He still smiles when we talk about it.

What happened to Reid is not uncommon when you set goals. We aren't born knowing what we can accomplish. We have to prove it to ourselves. When he began to set goals and realized he could do more than he originally thought possible, Reid began to get excited about setting new and higher goals. In fact he found that he was willing to do whatever it took to make his goals happen. He would skip breaks, stay later and so on. Without a goal, he would have settled for whatever happened, instead of pushing to make something bigger happen.

If setting goals can do this for a twelve-year-old boy, what can it do for you?!

### Gain More than Results with Goal Setting

Setting goals and doing what it takes to achieve those goals will give you new confidence and higher self-esteem. As your confidence grows, so will the size of your goals.

Like Reid, you want to set a goal that is a stretch. If he had set a goal to pick forty pounds when he had picked forty the day before, there wouldn't have been that incredible sense of accomplishment. If you already have four parties booked, don't set a goal to hold four parties. You're already there. Set a stretch goal, one that you'll have to work at to hit—one that will really give you that sense of "I did it!" Remember also that Reid didn't set a goal to pick ninety pounds when he'd picked sixty the day before. As his confidence, experience and skill grew, his goals increased gradually.

### Every Goal Needs a "Why"

Like Reid and Elizabeth, you want to set clear, attainable goals. If you aren't clear on what you want from your business, then anything will do. On the other hand, if you know what you want from your business, and even more importantly, why you want it, you are much more likely to succeed. For instance, if you decide that you want to earn $500 a month from your business so that you can buy new furniture for your living room, the $500 is your goal and the furniture is your "why."

Maybe you want to earn $600 per month so you can save $300 per month for a down payment on a new car and have $300 a month left to use for extras like treating the family to dinner, going out to a movie or buying new clothes without feeling guilty. Maybe your goal is even higher. Perhaps you want to set a goal to earn $1,000 a month so that you can save for a down payment on a home. Perhaps your goal might be simply to get out of the house once a week for adult conversation and chocolate!

The goal and the "why" will be different for everyone. The important thing is to have them—the goal, so that you have a target, since without a target anything will do, and the "why" because money by itself does not motivate us. What the money will do is to help us do or have something specific that we want.

> **It's never the money. It's what the money will do.**

Setting a goal, knowing your "why" and developing a plan to achieve your goal are the keys to your success. Like Reid, you may even find the sense of accomplishment you feel to be even more rewarding than your "why."

### How to Set Goals

The most powerful goals are S.M.A.R.T. goals. This system was originally developed back in 1981 by George T. Doran ("There's a S.M.A.R.T. way to write management's goals and objectives."). The initials can be interpreted in various ways. However, they are all close to the following, which is what I use:

**Specific:** For instance, "I want to sell a lot next month" is not specific. "I want to sell $1,000" is specific.

**Measurable:** At the end of the month you need to be able to measure your goal to see if you hit your target. If you sold $1,000, you hit your goal. If you sold $750, you missed your goal.

**Attainable:** You have to believe that your goal is attainable. If you don't, you won't make the effort. American author Napoleon Hill said, "Whatever the mind of man can conceive and believe it can achieve!"

**Realistic:** Your goal needs to be realistic. If your goal was to sell $10,000 this month, you might be setting yourself up to fail, which defeats the purpose of setting goals.

**Time frame:** A goal must have a time frame. "I want to sell $1,000 this month" has a specific time frame.

Here is a six-step goal-setting process that, when followed, will take you anywhere you want your business to go. I've provided a Sample Goals Worksheet as well as a S.M.A.R.T. Goals Template at the end of this chapter for your use.

**1. My goal is:** _____

Make this specific, measurable, attainable and realistic and set a deadline. Make it a S.M.A.R.T. goal. It could be how many parties you want to hold this month, how much you would like to earn this month or how many people you want to recruit. You could choose to set goals in some or all of these areas. You decide. The important thing is that they are *your* goals—not what someone else thinks you can or can't do. What do *you* want to accomplish? What would make *you* feel successful? Once you decide, write down your goal and congratulate yourself! You just did what only about one percent of all Americans do. You wrote down your goal. You will actually feel energized by taking this simple step of writing down your goal. You see, a dream not written down is just a wish. By putting your goal to print, you make a much stronger mental commitment.

**2. The benefit to me is:** _____

The next step is to list all the benefits to accomplishing your goal. The benefits are your "why." The more benefits there are, the more likely you are to do the work to achieve your goal. If your goal was to earn $500 this month, some of the benefits might be:

• To prove to myself that I could do it (Increased self-esteem)
• To be recognized for my sales at the monthly meeting
• To earn the incentive for that level of sales
• To take my family on a mini-vacation

It's really exciting when you stop and list all the benefits you will receive for accomplishing the goal, and your commitment to accomplishing your goal will be much stronger.

**3. Affirmation:** _____

An affirmation is the act of writing your goal as though it has already happened. It could sound like this: "I'm so glad I didn't give up on achieving my goal! I can't believe I earned enough money to buy all the school clothes the kids needed for the new school year. I am so proud of myself and my family is too! I told them I was being recognized tonight at the meeting for my sales achievement and they hugged and congratulated me. I even earned the logo tote bag!" Whenever you get discouraged, you can read your affirmation and it will bring you back to that original commitment level.

**4. Break it down:** Breaking your goal down into pieces that feel achievable is the last piece of getting personal buy-in on your goal. For instance, let's say your goal is to earn $500 and you earn a 25 percent commission on your sales. Therefore, you would have to sell $2,000 this month in order to reach that goal. That can feel like a pretty big number. Breaking it down will help make it feel achievable.

The process works like this—$2,000 in sales in thirty days is:
- $500 a week
- $67 a day
- Six parties this month
- An average of 1.5 parties a week
- One party every five days
- One party every 120 hours
- I could hold two parties on three Saturdays this month. Then I would only have to work three days this month!
- If a party takes me one-and-a-half to two hours from start to finish, I'd only be working nine to twelve hours this month to earn $500.

At what point did you think, "Oh, I can do that!"? That's the power of breaking down your goal!

**5. Action plan:** Now that you have broken down your goal to a point where it feels attainable to you, you are ready to create a step-by-step action plan to achieve your goal. An action plan might look something like this if the goal is $500 this month in income:

a. Create a contact list of people to call to book parties.

b. Schedule time each day to contact the names on my list to book parties.

c. Book one party a day for the next eight days. In order to hold six parties, I need to book eight to allow for cancellations.

d. Give or mail each hostess a hostess packet.

e. Effectively coach each hostess using the three-contact checklist for high attendance and minimal cancellations.

6. **Work the plan:** Many people get to Step 5 and then stop. An action plan only works if you work it! Look at your plan and schedule the actions you will need to make in your calendar in order to make that plan actually happen, resulting in reaching your goal!

## Visuals Are a Great Way to Stay Motivated and Focused

When I had a goal to earn the incentive trip to Hawaii, I kept the brochure the company had sent on my desk where I could see it all the time. I had a palm tree on my fridge that had different levels of points listed to the side. Every week I colored in the point level I had achieved. The brochure kept me motivated and the chart kept me focused and aware of how many points I needed to make my goal a reality.

When our kids were little we were planning a big trip—our first family cruise! We were hoping to take the trip that May. However, it would depend on how much we could save after bills each month. We put a thermometer on the fridge that had different dollar levels. The top level was what we needed to pay for the trip. We colored it in at the end of each month. How much we colored in each month depended on how much I earned. Coloring in that thermometer was a monthly highlight for the family as we watched it fill up.

We took the trip that May and had so much fun that we took a cruise every year after that for many years. Our kids never complained about Mom leaving to do a party, because they knew if I was gone, the chart would be fuller at the end of the month. Our youngest child Carli was eight years old the year we took that first cruise. She is 23 today. The other day I asked her if she remembered the family meetings we used to have. She said, "Not really, but I remember the thermometer!" Whatever your goal is, pictures are a powerful way to keep you motivated. Put the picture in a prominent place where you can see it every day and track your progress.

When you follow these steps, you will have taken some very important actions to ensure your success! By setting a goal, you really have made a promise to yourself to achieve something that is important to you. You will find that setting a goal and following the steps in this chapter will bring you success you never dreamed you could have. As you achieve *success on purpose*, you will find you have the confidence to set even higher goals and you will have the belief that you can achieve them!

Lastly, take words like *try*, or *hope*, or *we'll see what happens* out of your vocabulary! When you make statements like "I'm going to try to get bookings", or "I hope I can do this", or even "we'll see what happens", you are actually leaving yourself a back way out. What happens when we do that is that we usually take it!

Instead, say things like, "When I earn $1,000 this month", and "I have a plan and I'm going to work the plan and make sure it happens" or "I am so determined to hit my goal." These are empowering statements that can give you confidence just by saying them—even if you only say them to yourself.

I have been a consistent goal setter for years and years. However, I must tell you, there have been times when I did not hit my goal. I gave it everything I had and still missed the target. That happens to all of us. When that happens, we can say, "I failed" or we can say, "I never gave up! I missed the ultimate target, but I'm much further along than I would have been if I hadn't set the goal and committed wholeheartedly to it!"

Being goal-oriented is an essential characteristic of all high-achieving men and women in every field. It simply isn't possible to reach even a fraction of your potential until you have learned how to set and reach goals and make that a habit.

Paraphrasing famous oil billionaire H.L. Hunt, "In America, you only need two things to be successful: 1. Determine exactly what you want. 2. Determine the price you'll have to pay to get it and then resolve to pay that price!"

When you set a goal, you have to ask yourself this question: Do I want it bad enough to do whatever it takes to get it? I always wanted to play the piano well. I admired people who could sit down and play beautifully. I took lessons for a couple of years, but never really got to a place where I was any good at it. I finally had to admit to myself that I wasn't willing to practice enough to get good at it. I didn't want to do the work—I just wanted the result.

The skill of setting goals, having an attitude of commitment to those goals and a willingness to do what it takes to make your goals a reality will be one of the biggest keys to your success! If you haven't set some goals recently, set aside time now and make that happen. By doing so, you will set in motion the process of creating more and more success in your business and your life.

# S.M.A.R.T. Goals

*"Success on Purpose"*

### S.M.A.R.T. goals

**S**pecific – **M**easurable – **A**ttainable – **R**ealistic – **T**ime frame

1. My goal is: (specific with a time frame)

2. The benefit to me is:

3. Affirmation:

4. Break it down:
   1.
   2.
   3.
   4.
   5.
   6.
   7.

5. Action Plan:
   1.
   2.
   3.
   4.
   5.
   6.

6. Work the Plan!

## "Persistence = Results = ENTHUSIASM = BIGGER Results!"

## Sample - Goals Worksheet

*"Success on Purpose"*

S.M.A.R.T. goals:

**S**pecific – **M**easurable – **A**ttainable – **R**ealistic – **T**ime frame

### 1. My goal is: (specific with a time frame)

Earn $600 in my first month of business

### 2. The benefit to me is:

To prove to myself that I could do it.

Earn the incentive for new consultant sales.

Pay cash for school clothes

### 3. Affirmation:

I'm so glad I didn't give up on my goal! I can't believe I earned

enough money for the school clothes. I'm so proud of myself and

my family is too! I even earned the logo tote bag!

### 4. Break it down:

1) Hold six parties at $350 each

2) Hold one party every five days

3) Hold one party every 120 hours

4) Hold two parties on two Saturdays and one party on two weeknights. (work four days the whole month!)

5) Hold three parties on two Saturdays. (Work two days this month)

6) If a party takes one and a half to two hours from start to finish I will only be working 9-12 hours this month to earn $600!

7) Sell $450 per week to hit my goal.

### 5. Action Plan:

1) Create a contact list of 100 names.

2) Schedule time to contact the names on my list to schedule my first six parties.

3) Give or mail each hostess a hostess packet.

4) Complete "three-contacts" with each hostess.

5) Listen to ALL the segments on the Strong Start CD and complete accompanying segments in the workbook.

6) Practice my party presentation.

### 6. Work the Plan!

## "Persistence = Results = ENTHUSIASM = BIGGER Results!"

# 9: GETTING MORE BOOKINGS IN TODAY'S MARKET

This chapter is about how to get more bookings and fewer cancellations in today's market. Before we get to what *you* can do, I want to give you some background. It actually was through my team coaching, team mentoring and my personal coaching that I even realized that there was a shift in the market—yet again. It started when I was talking with one client who was having trouble filling her calendar. She's a long-time direct seller and never had any problems. When I worked with some of my other coaching clients throughout the next couple of weeks, I asked, "What do you want to talk about today? What are some of your struggles?"

I heard things like, "You know, Shari, it just feels like my calendar is falling apart. I never had so much difficulty booking parties." When I was on calls with my two team mentoring groups, I again asked, "What do you want to talk about today? What are some of the challenges you're facing?" Every single one of them said bookings. They couldn't get them, and the ones that they were getting were falling off their calendars. These are people from all over the country, all with different companies. When you hear that so frequently in a period of a couple of weeks, you know that something's going on out there.

As I began to brainstorm with my clients, we started to see a pattern. I have to thank my personal coaching clients and my team mentor groups for helping me to figure out what is going on in the market and how we can combat the challenge of getting more bookings now and avoiding cancellations.

## What's Really Happening in Our Market Today?

Let's talk about today's woman. She works full-time and has two children who are each engaged in three programs, to which she chauffeurs them. She cleans, she cooks, and she does the grocery shopping. She answers the phone, responds to emails, sends about 1500 text messages per month and spends about five hours per day on Facebook® and other social media venues. She is overwhelmed, stressed out and ready to tip over the edge.

When we ask today's woman if she would like to book a party, she thinks, "Are you crazy? I don't have time for that!" Even if someone books a party thinking that somehow she can make this all work with her schedule, she often quickly realizes that she just doesn't have time for this. She feels even more overwhelmed. When this happens, what's the one thing that she is going to cut out of her schedule? It's not her children's programs, and trust me, it's not Facebook and it's not texting. It's your party. That's why the cancellations are coming in.

The challenge right now, I really believe, is that women are just completely overwhelmed and the idea of putting something else on their plates is just not very attractive, no matter how fabulous your products are or how much free product she might get. I don't believe this challenge is going to go away. The answer is really clear and simple: These women feel that hosting a party is *adding* something to their plates and they simply can't fathom doing that. We've got to make them feel like hosting parties is taking something *off* their

plates. Let's see how just using different verbiage can cl
they will perceive having a party.

Look at the next two scripts and ask yourself which would make you
say yes to hosting a party:

**Script 1.**
**You:** Is Cindy in?
**Cindy:** This is Cindy
**You:** Hi, Cindy. This is Shari with XYZ Company. Do you have a few
minutes to talk? I have some really exciting news to share with you!
**Cindy:** Sure, I have just a few before I have to start dinner.
**You:** No problem, this will take just a few minutes. I wanted to let
you know that the (product) that you love so much is 75 percent off
to our hostesses this month, plus all the free product and half-priced
items you always receive. What do you think? Would you like to take
advantage of that?

**Script 2.**
**You:** Is Cindy in?
**Cindy:** This is Cindy
**You:** Hi Cindy, this is Shari with XYZ Company. Do you have just a
few minutes?
**Cindy:** Sure, I have just a few before I have to start dinner.
**You:** Wonderful! Thank you for taking the time to talk with me. I
know how busy you are. In fact that's actually the reason I am calling.
I've had so many people at my parties lately tell me how nice it was
to take a break from the chaos of their lives and enjoy a night off
with girlfriends. It made me realize that we as women are always
on the run, never taking time for ourselves. So I've been calling all
my best customers and past hostesses to ask how long it's been since
they had a night off with their girlfriends. What do you think, Cindy,

would you enjoy a break from the madness, a glass of wine with your girlfriends and a little shopping?

Did you almost sigh as you read the second script? Did you think, "Yes! I want a glass of wine and some girlfriend time."?

I have been teaching this verbiage for a while now and it works beautifully. The people who have used it have full calendars once again. We're asking them to do the same thing in both scripts, but it feels entirely different.

Free product today is not reason enough for a woman to add more to her already full plate. Taking a break from the chaos and escaping the madness feels like you are helping her take something off her plate. This verbiage is working incredibly well with the people that I'm training. They are getting lots of bookings using this approach—on their booking calls, as well as on Facebook—which we're going to talk about in Part Three of this book.

This language works great at parties as well. You are reminding them that this is a break by just mentioning, "Isn't it nice to take a break from all the madness of our lives and just enjoy some girlfriend time like you're doing tonight?" Those consultants who have used this approach are finding that it is easily getting them bookings from their parties, and it is keeping those booked hostesses from canceling.

"Aren't you excited to take a break from everything and just get together with your girlfriends? Oh my goodness! Your girlfriends are just going to love you for giving them this escape from all the chaos. It's going to be so much fun to just have some wine and some girlfriend time." Use this phraseology in all the different phases of your work: hostess coaching, bookings on the phone, on Facebook and at your parties as well.

One last point: When using this approach at a party, make sure you keep your presentation short. Today's woman is going to give you thirty minutes to present and then she's going to start to get fussy. You'll see her start to cross her arms, fidget in her chair and glance at her watch. You'll see her facial expression start to change. If you go over thirty minutes in your presentation, your bookings and your sales will suffer. Therefore, let's get that party presentation down to thirty minutes.

To summarize, the key phrases that work today are:

1. Take a break from the madness

2. Escape the chaos

3. Take a night off

## Making the Shift to "Fun, Fast and Easy"

Today, more than ever, we need to make hosting a party fun, fast and easy. Fun, fast and easy is what you've got to really focus on these days in order to book more parties and to keep more parties on your calendar. Make booking the party—on the phone, on Facebook or wherever you book your parties—fun, fast and easy. Make the process of hosting a party fun, fast and easy. Make the actual presentation itself fun, fast and easy so that when you're at the party, you're getting multiple bookings from that party. This is the key to having your business grow and thrive in the 21st century.

## Setting the Stage for Better Booking Results

Before you start to make those booking contacts, send out an email to your customer base, including your past hostesses, that says, "Earning free product is faster, easier, and more fun than ever." Then just list some of the things that you're doing today to make this possible. You could even say something like, "We know today's woman is busier than any woman in the last century. I want to make hosting a party easier, faster, and more fun for you. Here are some of the new things that I'm doing to make that possible."

You could list a few things from the next chapter, "Theme Parties Generate Lots of Fun and Sales." You could mention the restaurant party, the co-host idea, the stop and shop, the 5-1-1 party, or one of the other theme party ideas. Send this out before you start making your booking contacts. What you do not want to do is call and say, "Hi Mary. This is Shari with XYZ Company. I've got so many things I want to tell you about that are going to make hosting parties faster, more fun, and easier for you." If you just start spieling off ten different things that you can do to make it fun, fast and easy for them, it will completely overwhelm them. What you can do is to send out an email to look over before you call, giving them lots of different ideas about how they can have a party today in a more fun way, an easier way and a faster way.

## Booking Calls as Follow-Up to that Email Message

If you are following up on the phone, the call could sound something like this, "Hi Jenny. It's Shari with XYZ Company. Do you have just a few minutes? Thanks Jenny. I sent out an email two days ago to all of my best hostesses." That's important. It will make her feel special, even though you sent it to everyone. "You know, I'm noticing more and more that women today seem to be getting busier and busier. Very few women are taking time for themselves to have some fun time with their girlfriends. As you can see from my email, I'm doing some really unique kinds of parties. These parties all focus on easy ways to have fun with your friends, like a restaurant party or a stop and shop. Did either of these or one of the other types of parties I sent to you pique your interest?"

Notice that I just mentioned a couple of ideas. If you know this person fairly well, you probably know what two party formats might appeal to her, and those are the ones you will mention. If you don't know, just pick a couple of your favorites. Did you see that I also said, "or did one of the other types of parties I sent to you pique your interest?" Maybe there was one that caught her eye that she can mention at that point in the call.

Remember that the confused mind just says no. Sending out the email first sets the stage for everything being fun, fast and easy. Following up will really make a difference in your bookings.

## Using Texting as a Business Tool

Now, let's talk about another platform for booking parties, for hostess coaching and for recruiting. Not too long ago, my friend Barbie Collins Young and I were talking on the telephone. She shared with me something that her entire region had tested with fantastic results. I was all ears. What she started to share with me was so totally outside my box and outside of the way I've trained forever, that I was resistant. However, when she was done talking, it really made a lot of sense to me.

What she told me was that her entire leader team in her region did a little test with texting. The people they targeted were those they couldn't reach by phone, who had said they wanted to have parties and even people who had booked parties. They were also people who said they were interested in the business opportunity but were not responding to phone calls. Barbie's leaders were leaving messages, they were calling back frequently, sending emails and just not getting any response. So they decided, for those people that were not responding, that they would text them! The results were unbelievable across the board. They got instant responses from hostesses, potential hostesses and potential recruits. Their booking parties went crazy, and they were recruiting people very quickly. It was really, really working. As I considered this, I thought, "Would I rather pick up the phone and answer a phone call or would I rather respond to a text?" How about you? Would you rather answer a phone call or respond to a text? It made perfect sense. From that point on I have been training my clients on using this tool, as well as sharing about it on my teleconference calls, and it is working beautifully.

I'm going to challenge you to use texting when connecting with people who have expressed interest in booking a party, with hostesses who are not responding and with people who have expressed interest in the business opportunity. It's not a tool for generating interest. If it's someone who is already interested, this is a great way to connect with her.

For a tool that you can use to generate lots of interest, see the chapter on "Using Facebook for Better Booking and Sponsoring Results" on page 157.

Review this chapter carefully and see how you want to incorporate these tools into your day-to-day business efforts. You may find that you are able to get better and better results in less and less time. In this day and age, that is definitely a good thing!

# 10: ENSURING SUCCESSFUL PARTIES IN TODAY'S MARKET

In dealing with today's market, the first order of business is to make it easy to host parties. There are a number of things you can do to make things easy and fun for your hostess. Doing these will make it easy for your hostess, ensure good attendance and make it less likely that she will cancel.

**1. More important than ever is to help your hostess create a guest list.** Don't put a template handout in her hostess package that says, "List your friends, relatives, acquaintances, neighbors and kid contacts," with a list of fifty blank slots that she can fill in. She just won't do it. She's too busy, even if she has good intentions. Instead, take the time to help her create a list. You can say, "Okay Mary, can you think of three friends? Wonderful. Write those down. Can you think of three relatives?" Go for three in each category. Now she has fifteen names on the list. Go back and mix it up. "Great, that's wonderful. Can you think of three friends' relatives? Great! Go ahead and write those down. How about three relatives' friends, your mom's best friend, your sister's coworker, and so on?"

Keep mixing it up until she has a list of forty or fifty names. It won't take you any more than five or ten minutes and she will have a nice list of people to invite. If you don't do this, she will write down ten names or send a mass email to her friends and you know what that means—a sure disaster.

Even if you are using Facebook® with this hostess (see "Coaching Your Hostess Using Facebook" on page 167), mail out the postcards for her. I know that doing this may not be your favorite thing—there is an expense tied to mailing out the postcards and it's a time-consuming task for you. However, parties are where everything comes from, right? Your bookings, your commissions, your future customers, your future hostesses, your sponsors, your future leaders, your sales all come from parties.

The more people you have at your parties, the more of everything you get. Even though the hostess may have sent out an email invite, if you mail out those postcards, for every twenty that you mail, you'll have three more attendees. If you don't mail the postcards, you will have three less attendees. Having a postcard to put on their fridge and look at every day reminds them about the upcoming party. People get so many emails, so many texts, so many Facebook invitations that the invite to your party could easily get lost in the shuffle. I know we're a techie world today. However, a piece of paper to put on the fridge is a better reminder that there's a party coming up, and it will increase your attendance. If you have three more attendees and they order $50 worth of product each, that's $150 in sales that you wouldn't get if you didn't mail out the postcards. Isn't that worth the time and expense?

**2. Encourage your hostess to make simple, easy snacks.** As the party gets closer and closer, the hostess begins to think about the food! She thinks that she has to make a cake and some kind of hors d'oeuvres, pick up wine or provide coffee and other beverages. It can start to overwhelm her, and is another reason for her to cancel. It will also discourage future bookings from her party. If she's got a fabulous spread, lots of different hors d'oeuvres, different kinds of wine and cocktails plus dessert, everybody will have a great time.

However, it's definitely going to hurt your bookings. Her guests will see how much she did and be wary of having to do that themselves. It can also influence or impact the number of cancellations you get. So, make sure that you're always encouraging her to keep her snacks simple, even giving her some ideas of what simple snacks might look like, such as cookies and tea, or some cheese and crackers and wine.

**3. Help your hostess create her wish list.** Today, more than ever, a wish list is critical. On the second contact with your hostess, ask her if she's got her wish list for you, because you're dying to know what she wants for herself. If she says, "Oh, I haven't really got into that yet," stop everything and help her create a wish list. This is her "why." You know that in the direct selling business, it's never the money—it's what the money will do. When we tie income to something tangible that we could get from that income, then it becomes important to us. It's the same with your hostess.

You can say our average hostess receives $100 of free product and two half-priced items. However, if she doesn't tie that to something tangible, it very quickly becomes something she can do later when she's not so busy. What usually happens is it just keeps getting put off and put off and put off. As soon as she ties that free product, half-priced items and hostess specials (or your offers for that month) to something that she really wants, the party becomes much more urgent for her. She can't wait to get that great serving bowl. She can't wait to get the crystal necklace and earring set and wear it to that special event coming up.

Whatever your product, when you have your hostess get clear about what she wants, it becomes much more important to her, much more real and much more urgent. Now, she doesn't want to wait until next month to get it. She's anxious to have her party so she can get it now and maybe get it free! If she hasn't created a wish list, stop everything right now! Say something like this, "Well, gosh, pull out your catalog and let's go through it together. I want to know what you want to get free so I can tell you exactly what we have to have in sales at your party to make sure we get that for you." Walk her through the catalog and create her wish list with her.

**4. Keep coaching calls short and to the point.** Time is an issue here. Don't go off into social conversation. Don't ask about the family and all those kinds of things. In respect for her time, keep your coaching short and to the point. You need to cover certain things in your coaching in order to have a successful party. Also, do not do this coaching in person. You don't have the time; they don't have the time. More than ever, that just doesn't work. Remember that you're trying to keep it fun, fast and easy. Coach over the phone—it's easier for you and it's easier for her. Keep those calls short and to the point.

**5. Remind her on every single call what she's getting for hosting her party.** When you ask your hostess if she remembers what she is getting for hosting that party, the most likely answer is no! Tell her again, and that will keep it fresh and exciting in her mind. Also, talk about the fun that she's going to have at her party, what you are going to do to make sure that her guests have fun, how it's going to be a great evening—great girlfriend time – a wonderful night off for everyone. Keep her excited about the benefits to her for hosting a party. The fun part is just as important as the free product.

**6. Build rapport and relationship with your hostess.** The better your rapport, the harder it will be for a hostess to cancel a party. If she likes you and you have good rapport with her, it's much harder for her to cancel than if she doesn't have a relationship with you. Building rapport with her starts at the party where you met and extends over the period of time that you work with her. When you first meet someone at a party, use the time before the party starts, during the presentation and during shopping time to build rapport with your guests and to start building relationships.

When you're on the phone with your hostess, talk about how you want to make sure that she has the best party in the neighborhood, the best party of all of her—or your—friends. Say things like, "You're so easy to work with!" "Gosh, you're just a delight, Jill." Compliment her, call her by name and keep her the center of attention, the center of focus in all of your coaching.

Avoid straying into social conversation. Certainly, if she mentions that her son is sick today you want to respond. "Oh gosh, is he okay? What's the problem?" More importantly, it's just keeping her the center of focus, always complimenting her, telling her how great she is. Make sure you praise her on everything she does well, always call her by name and make sure that in your language, the focus is always on how concerned and committed you are to making sure that she has a fabulous party, that her friends have a ton of fun, and that she gets a lot of free products. The focus is on her. Those are all rapport and relationship builders.

**7. Keep the focus on fun and friendship during your coaching calls.** The number one reason people have parties is to have fun. Nobody has the friendship time that they want today, myself included. How about you? Are you getting together with your girlfriends as much as you would like or does the week just pass by? Then the month just passes by. All of a sudden, it's been three months since you've done anything with your girlfriends, or gone out to dinner with your sister. Keep the fun and friendship in front of them, and keep the pain of not having that in front of them by saying things like, "I'm so excited about your party. You said it's been three months since you've been with your girlfriends. This is going to be so good for you, all of you getting together."

**8. Support them in doing their own reminder calls.** This is a little different focus than what I've been saying all along as far as making it fun, fast and easy for your hostesses. One of the things that some consultants start to do when RSVPs start to drop or when the hostess shows resistance to making reminder calls, is to say, "Well, I'll do it for you." If you are doing one party a month, you may have time to do that. However, making reminder calls for even four parties a month, with ten people who have confirmed yes for each party, is forty additional phone calls every month. You don't have time for that. There are better ways for you to spend your time. You can get the hostess to do that. It's just about using the right language.

This is one of the places where hostesses are very resistant. They feel like they are bugging their guests. Here's what you can say: "I understand that. However, I can promise you that if you make your reminder calls tonight, you're going to have more guests at your party tomorrow. Tell me if this feels a little bit more comfortable to you than just 'Hey, I want to remind you about the party tomorrow.' What if you said, 'Hi Mom, it's Sue. I'm getting my snacks together for my party tomorrow night, and I want to check and see if you were bringing a friend.' You've reminded her about your party and that she can bring her friend. All she probably heard was that you just want to make sure you have enough snacks for all the people who are coming."

Set each hostess up this way to make those reminder calls the night before the party. You will have her feeling more comfortable and the calls will get made. This will ensure better attendance and lessen the likelihood of the party being canceled.

As a side note, I don't want you to be confused as we talk about the different platforms to use in regard to phone, email, text and Facebook. Facebook is the most effective way to reach and connect with hostesses and guests today. Texting is second, email is third and the phone is number four. However, you will have different customers who prefer different ways of communication. One might prefer the phone while another prefers Facebook. I want you to understand the tools to use to effectively work with all of your customers, using their preferred mode of communication.

## What Can We Do at Our Parties to Have Them Be Fun, Fast and Easy?

The key here is making our presentation fun, fast and easy. This will ensure good sales and multiple bookings. Making a "fast" presentation is going to be tough for some people and easier for others. Some companies have gotten the presentation down to sixty minutes. That's actually the language that I hear from them, "we've got them down from two hours to sixty minutes." Sorry, an hour or longer presentation is not going to work in today's market.

Your presentation has to be about thirty minutes. Anything past that and you will lose their attention and they will resent having less social time. Remember that they are so busy, overwhelmed, stressed and exhausted that when they commit to come to a party, all they want is social time. They want to visit, they want to relax, they want some girlfriend time and they want some "me" time. That's what they're there for. It's the one day this month, maybe this quarter that they are going to get that downtime.

Anything longer than thirty minutes or so, and you will start to kill the rapport and the relationships that you've worked to build before the presentation started. You're going to hurt your bookings because they won't want to invite their friends to sit through another forty-five-minute or hour-long presentation. If it's fun, fast and easy, you're going to get more bookings, they're going to have more fun and you're going to have a stronger rapport than if they had to listen to an hour-long presentation.

Besides keeping your presentation short, it needs to be engaging. You can find some great ideas on doing this in the chapter, "Booking Parties at Parties" that starts on page 133.

Lastly, don't be rigid about how your routine goes. Some companies advise, "First do this, then do this, then do this, and then serve snacks and drinks." We are operating in a different world today. The guests and the hostess are stressed out, overwhelmed and tired. They are there for fun. Give them food, give them drinks, whether it's soft drinks or wine or margaritas. If your hostess wants to have refreshments before your presentation—no problem. If she wants to have them afterwards—no problem. Go with her timeline and you will have a happier hostess and happier guests.

The bottom line to this chapter is that today's market requires that you make some shifts in how you do your business. Look and see how you can implement the above ideas quickly and easily. Then look forward to having consistently successful parties and having your business grow despite busy schedules and economic challenges.

# 11: THEME PARTIES GENERATE LOTS OF FUN AND SALES

I am a huge fan of theme parties, especially in the current market. What I've learned over many years in this industry is that theme parties increase attendance. Would you rather attend a home décor party or a Mexican fiesta? Would you rather attend a candle party or a Naughty Nightie party where everybody brings their nighties in brown paper bags and you pull them out throughout the evening, with everyone guessing which nightie belongs to which guest? Would you rather attend a cooking or tasting party or a pajama party where everybody comes in their PJs and enjoys a glass of wine and tastes some great food? What sounds like more fun? Theme parties are more casual, fun and relaxed. Remember that in today's market, the more you can do to make parties fun, fast and easy, the more successful you will be.

## Get More Bookings and Fewer Cancellations

Offering theme parties will, more than ever, help you to book and keep more parties. The attendance will be higher because people are clearly coming to have fun. The guests may have confirmed, and the hostess may think she is going to have great attendance. However, at the last minute, people call and cancel or just don't show up. I recently spoke with a coaching client who had a party scheduled, the hostess sent out sixty invitations and one guest attended. Granted, there may have been a breakdown in the follow-up/reminder process. However, if that had been a theme party, do you think that she might have had more attendance than if guests just received an offer to come and see her product? Theme parties are great ways to add an element of fun to your parties, keep attendance up and minimize cancellations.

## Where to Find Ideas for Theme Parties

Think about what's going on in a particular month. Let's take a look at May. What about a mother/daughter party before Mother's Day? You could also do something related to Memorial Day—see the comment below about July 4th. June is a big month for graduations and weddings—and don't forget Father's Day. How can you tie weddings and Father's Day into your parties and make everything fun, fast and easy? What can you do to tie that theme back to your product in a fun, fast and easy way?

In July, we have the Fourth of July. That's easy. Consider red, white, and blue parties with cheesecake topped with strawberries, blueberries and whipped cream. In August, your hostesses may be dealing with back-to-school shopping. It's a chance for those moms to get out with some girlfriends in that hectic time when it's all about shopping for pencils and school clothes. In June, July and August, you can talk about deck parties or even pool parties. Pool parties in most of the country are a lot of fun. You just have a party around your pool. In Washington, we don't get enough sun to justify owning a pool, so our pool parties were centered on a little kiddy pool filled with ice, sodas, wine coolers, bottles of wine and beer or whatever. Was that fun? Was that silly? Absolutely. However, it was also fun, fast and easy. In September, the kids are back in school so you might suggest a "Yeah! The Kids Are Back In School" party.

## Take the Party Out of the Home

There are a number of venues where you can hold parties that are not in someone's home. What about a park party? That's a fun, fast and easy way to do a party when the weather is nice. This can work great with a hostess who has a park near her house. You get your product there, the kids can play and everyone gets some girlfriend time—fun, fast and easy. Remember, the number one reason people book parties today is fun.

A restaurant party is another great way to make a party fun, fast and easy. The last time I was in the field, I did a restaurant party nearly every week. Why did I do a restaurant party every week? Whenever I talked about it at my parties, I would always say, "I do at least one of these every week." It's funny when you say things like that. The guests would think, "It's a great idea because if she's doing one a week, everybody must love it." You talk about fun, fast and easy! The guests arrive after work. You can have the party start at 5-5:30 p.m. and be over in time for people to still have a nice amount of time at home that evening.

As people arrive, they each order a glass of wine or something else to drink and maybe some appetizers. By the way, each guest pays for her own food and drink. You don't buy it, and the hostess doesn't buy it. You don't want this to be a big expense for you or the hostess. Since people are coming right from work, there is no chance they are going to get caught up with something at home and not get out the door. The whole evening is set up as quick and easy girlfriend time with no formal presentation. All you need to do is put your product in the middle of the table, meander around the table, answer questions, get people catalogs and take orders. You're in and out in an hour to an hour and a half—fun, fast and easy.

## Not a Theme But Still Fun, Fast and Easy

A great way to make any kind of party fun, fast and easy is for two friends to host a party together. They share the responsibility with one providing her home, and the other bringing the snacks. Also, you have two people inviting guests, which means there are likely to be a lot more people there than with just one hostess. With this scenario, the two hostesses share the free product.

A "Stop and Shop" party is great for offices. You go to an office at lunchtime or right after work, and set up in the lunchroom or in a conference room. You've got a captive audience and the employees can do a potluck or just order pizza. Make it easy—and that makes it fun. You're in and out in about an hour, especially if it's a lunchtime party.

Another approach is a 5-1-1 party. This idea is from Mary Overton, a top seller in her company. When we talk about fast, fun and easy, a 5-1-1 party is exactly that. What you do is have the prospective hostess commit to have five confirmed guests for her party. Then have those five guests commit to bringing one guest each. That gives you ten guests. Then commit to a one-hour party. Arrive and depart in a one-hour time frame. You can tell your hostess on the phone that you're doing something new—that you're going to be in and out in one hour. You're going to make it easier for her guests to say yes to attending, and you're going to make it easier for everyone to have the bulk of their evening ahead of them. Of course, their guests can stay and visit. Is that fun, is that fast, is it easy? Absolutely!

Getting away from the standard direct selling industry party is a really good idea. Besides the fact that a theme party or a different location will create more interest and higher attendance, you, as the consultant, get a reputation for creating fun experiences. Your hostesses and their guests will love you for it and book more parties! Which of the above ideas are you going to try next?

# 12: MAKING AN EFFECTIVE BOOKING CALL

There are definitely market trends in our business. There are times every year when it's very easy to book parties and there are times when it is much harder to fill our calendar. That's just part of our business. What I've noticed is that there are always consultants who have a full calendar regardless of the month, and there are those who see a problem with any month. They say things like, "It's January, and nobody has any money. It's February, and everybody is saving money for Valentine's Day. It's March, and Spring breaks are going on—nobody wants to book this month. It's April and, with Easter this month, everybody has family stuff going on. It's May, and school is getting out and graduations are happening so nobody will book. It's June, and there are so many weddings, everybody is too busy. It's July, and everyone has family vacations so nobody will book. It's August, and everyone is spending their money on back to school stuff. It's September, and everybody is busy with school activities. It's October and with Halloween this month, everybody is busy decorating and going to Halloween parties. It's November, and with Thanksgiving this month, people are out of town for the holidays and nobody will book a party. It's December, and everybody is too busy shopping, decorating, and attending Christmas events to book a party."

If we want to, we can always find a reason not to book parties. The truth is that every month there are many, many people who will book! We just need to find them. Learning how to make an effective booking call will make that much easier!

### When is the Best Time of Day to Make Booking Calls?

I always found that I reached more people in the evening hours than during the day. I generally made my calls between six and eight in the evening on the nights I didn't have parties. Saturday and Sunday afternoons are good as well. Talking person-to-person will always get better results than voicemail. I also found that when I called a customer shortly after she received her product from a party she had attended, I had a better chance of getting a booking. She was more excited about the product than she would have been before she received it. I would ask if she had received her product and how she liked it. Then we would talk about how she could get more of the things she had not ordered at the party for free!

### Getting Past, "I'm too Busy"

One of the most common objections consultants hear when they are making their booking calls is, "I'm just too busy to have a party right now, but maybe later." How can we get our prospective hostess past that? It's true that people are busier today than they've been before. That's definitely a common objection, even though there are many others we'll hear when making our booking calls. We want to make the benefit of hosting a party more important to the prospective hostess than the effort it will take her to host. One of the most common mistakes we make is to make a booking call that sounds like this:

**Shari:** Ring, ring.
**Jill:** "Hello."
**Shari:** "Is Jill in?"
**Jill:** "This is Jill."

**Shari:** "Hi Jill. This is Shari with XYZ company. I met you at Leah's party the other night. I just wanted to call to see if you would be interested in hosting a party and receiving free product."

**Jill:** "Oh, I'd love to, but I'm so busy right now. Could you call me next month?"

**Shari:** "Sure, I'd love to."

Then we call next month and it goes something like this:

**Shari:** Ring, ring.

**Jill:** "Hello."

**Shari:** "Is Jill in?"

**Jill:** "This is Jill."

**Shari:** "Hi Jill. This is Shari. You asked me to follow up with you this month to see if this might be a better time for you to host a party."

**Jill:** "Oh, I'd love to, but things are crazy this month. Could you call me back next month?"

**Shari:** "Of course, I'd be happy to."

Then we call next month and it goes something like this:

**Shari:** Ring, ring.

**Jill:** "Hello."

**Shari:** "Is Jill in?"

**Jill:** "This is Jill."

**Shari:** "Hi Jill, this is Shari. You asked me to follow up with you this month to see if this might be a better time for you to host a party."

**Jill:** "Oh, I'd love to but I'm still so busy right now. Could you call me back next month?"

**Shari:** "Absolutely!"(We say with our happy face on!)

This can go on forever. The problem is we haven't put any sense of urgency in our invitation to host a party. There wasn't any reason to do it right away, so she could easily put it off until next month!

Remember, we want to make the benefit of hosting a party more important to our prospective hostess than the effort it will take her to host. How do we do that? That's a great question. The answer is one of the keys to making a successful booking call.

Before I share that key, it might be helpful for you to know the three top reasons people book parties today:

**3.** To help a friend

**2.** To get free product

**1.** To have fun!

## Know What Will Appeal to Each Prospective Hostess

Before you pick up the phone, take a moment to think about what benefit would most likely appeal to the individual you are about to call. Is there a particular product she would like to earn? Is she social and a person who would love the idea of getting a bunch of girlfriends together? Does she like to fuss over people and entertain? Does she need a break? These are just a few reasons that might make the benefit bigger than the effort. Focusing on what's in it for the hostess and getting her excited about the benefit to her will also minimize your cancellation rate.

There is one other thing to be conscious of when making booking calls. Let me ask you a question: Do you have time in your day for a twenty- or thirty-minute unexpected phone call, or are your days crammed full from the time you get up in the morning until the time you go to bed? Exactly! Few of us have time in our day for an unexpected phone call, and neither does our prospective hostess. We want to keep our call short and to the point. Here's a little tip: they know why you're calling. So why do we feel like we have to warm up the conversation by asking about the husband, the kids, the dog, the weather?

## Keep Your Call Short by Using the Short Script

In respect of our prospective hostess's time, we need to keep our booking calls short and to the point! That will allow you to make a booking call in about three to four minutes. Really! That means completing more calls in a shorter period of time and with better results. That means less phone time and more family time. Let's go over the short script together. There are six areas to the short script:

- Introduction
- Permission
- Purpose
- Benefit
- Objections
- Close

Let's briefly walk through how the script works:

**Introduction.** An example would be, "Hi Cindy, this is Shari with XYZ Company. I met you at Nikki's party the other night."

**Permission.** Ask if this is a good time. If she is in the middle of something, you won't have her full attention. You can say something like, "Do you have just a few minutes?"

**Purpose.** "I'd love to tell you about something I think you'll be really excited about."

**Benefit.** Tell her what you think she'll be excited about: a particular product, a special that's going on, free products, girlfriend time, paying off her new furniture. Remember to think about the biggest benefit to her before you pick up the phone.

**Objections.** When you ask if she'd like to book a party, she will more than likely have an objection. Our normal reaction is to go right into solving her problem. Sometimes we even do that in a way that can feel like we're arguing or challenging her objection. For instance, your prospective hostess might say, "Oh, no, I can't. I'm too busy." If you respond with something like, "You know, it actually doesn't take much time at all," or "I'm sure we can find a few hours in your schedule to have a party," she may feel that you are arguing with her. Instead, when someone gives you an objection, pause. This tells her you are listening to her and that you genuinely hear the concern. You'll also want to purposely slow down your speech and soften your tone. It will make her more receptive to your response.

Then try using the feel, felt, found technique. She'll be more receptive to your solutions when you do this. You can say, "I know how you feel, I felt that way before, and what I found was . . . " Then you can offer a possible solution. However, the feel, felt, found technique is a very old and well-used technique, and many people are familiar with it. Just change the wording a little. Instead you might say, "I understand how you feel. I've heard that from so many hostesses lately. Some of my hostesses have held parties at a restaurant or at work during lunchtime or right after work. That way they still had a fun time with friends and earned free product without having to take the time to get the house ready or prepare snacks. Would that be something that might work for you?"

You'll also want to soften your tone. Tone is as important as the words you use. You'll also notice that I said, "I don't know if this helps or not." Those simple words break down resistance immediately. What I am saying is I don't know if this is a solution. It is merely a suggestion, so they are receptive to it.

See the sample scripts below, as well as the Overcoming Today's Most Common Booking Objections section towards the end of this chapter, for how to address some common objections.

**Close.** Once you have answered her objections, ask for the date. Do it now while you have her attention and interest.

Here is an example of what a short script might sound like:

**Shari:** Ring, ring.

**Mary:** "Hello."

**Shari:** "Is Mary in?"

**Mary:** "This is Mary."

**Shari:** "Hi Mary, this is Shari. I met you at Lynn's birthday party the other day."

**Mary:** "Oh, sure. I remember you, Shari."

**Shari:** "Great! I wonder if I could take just a few minutes of your time."

**Mary:** "Sure I have just a few minutes. Then I have to start dinner."

**Shari:** "Thanks Mary. I promise to be brief. I want to tell you about something that I think you'll love."

**Mary:** "Sure, go ahead."

**Shari:** "I could tell that you and Lynn's other coworkers are a pretty close group. You guys have a lot of fun together, don't you?"

**Mary:** "Oh, yes, they're a really great group!"

**Shari:** "You mentioned how nice it was to take a break from all the chaos of life and get together with your girlfriends for a couple of hours. Why not host a party yourself in a couple weeks and do it again? You'd get another night with your friends and some great free product! What do you think?"

**Mary:** "You know Shari that really does sound like fun. We've always had a blast when we get together. But honestly, I live in a really tiny house. It's just too small to entertain in."

Pause . . . soften your tone and slow down.

**Shari:** "I understand. I know many people who feel the same way. I don't know if this helps or not, but I've noticed that sometimes when I do parties at big homes and the guests are spread out, the room is kind of quiet. It seems like when the room is smaller and the people are sitting close together they talk more and the party is noisier, more energetic and fun."

**Mary:** "That's true. I never thought of it that way."

**Shari:** "Would you like to go ahead and schedule a party with your friends? I just know you'll have a great time."

**Mary:** "Okay, sure."

**Shari:** "Oh good! I have Thursday the 28th and Tuesday the 19th. Which one works best for you?"

**Mary:** "Tuesday the 19th works great."

**Shari:** "Okay, I've got you down for Tuesday the 19th. I'm going to send you a hostess packet. I'll follow up in a couple of days to make sure you received it. In the meantime, go ahead and start creating your guest list. Your coworkers, of course, and don't forget family and friends."

**Mary:** "Ok, I'll start on the list and talk to you in a couple days."

**Shari:** "Great! When I call you to follow up on Wednesday, is one o'clock a good time?"

**Mary:** "That would be fine."

**Shari:** "Great, I'll talk to you at one on Wednesday. Thank you for scheduling a party, Mary! I really appreciate it."

**Mary:** "You're welcome, Shari."

**Shari:** "Okay, talk with you in a couple of days, Mary. Bye."


Now, if you timed that call, you would find that it takes about three minutes. The beauty of using the short script is that you can make five or six booking calls in as little as thirty minutes! Did you also notice that I scheduled our next call to avoid playing phone tag? The short script helps you maximize your time. You'll want to schedule a block of time to make calls. The idea is that when we do the same thing over and over for a block of time, we get into a routine and establish patterns. This concept works when doing your phone calls as well. When we make a booking call in the morning, one in the afternoon, and then one in the evening, we don't ever mentally get into a scheduling mode. So try setting aside one hour, or even thirty minutes, to make just booking calls. When you spend a concentrated amount of time on that one type of call, you'll find you get in a zone, and the conversation flows much better, with better results.

The last five years I was in the field, I held between 150 and 175 parties per year. I made booking calls for two hours a couple of times each week. Even with making that many booking calls, I found that the first two to three calls I did were all over the place. I wasn't in my zone yet, and often I couldn't think of what to say next or how to answer an objection. By the fourth call, I was in my zone! I'd make my first three booking calls to people I was pretty sure would say 'no', so that by the time I got to the good prospects, I was in my booking zone.

The other big benefit to the short script is that you won't overwhelm your prospective hostess with information! When we are excited about what we have to offer, it's easy to want to tell the person on the other end of the phone everything! It might sound something like this:

"Hi Jen, I met you at Susie's party the other night, but there were so many people there and I didn't get a chance to talk to you and I wanted to be sure you knew that you could get free product for having a party! I mean I mentioned it during the party, but it was kind of noisy and I wasn't sure people heard me talk about our hostess plan. Did you hear me say that you can get free product based on your sales, and half priced items depending on your sales, and we have a special incentive for hostesses this month, and I even offer extras for bookings? They have to hold, but once they hold, I do offer a special incentive, and we have a special recruiting incentive this month too, so if you're interested we could talk about how you can make money as a consultant, and earn free product and prizes! Oh and you'll love our team! You can meet them at the next meeting! So what do you think? Do you want to book a party or sign up?"

If we could see their face, we would probably see that "deer in headlights" expression! When people don't understand what you are saying, they just say no! The confused mind always says no. This is a booking call, not a hostess coaching call. You can explain the hostess plan during hostess coaching. In booking calls, like any other part of our business, we want to *make it easy to say yes*. You might even want to write those six words on an index card and keep it by your phone. By using the short script and keeping the focus on what's in it for them, you'll keep it appealing, simple, and easy to understand. When what you are offering is appealing, simple, and easy to understand, more people will say yes!

### Easy as 1-2-3-4!
To recap:
- Think about what would excite the prospective hostess to schedule a party before you pick up the phone.
- Keep the conversations short and to the point, using your short script.
- Answer objections using the *feel, felt, found* technique.
- Ask for the date, and make sure to thank the hostess for booking a party.

### Overcoming Today's Most Common Booking Objections
Here are some additional objections that you might come across in your booking conversations:

**Objection:** "I don't want to ask my friends to spend money right now."
**Response:** "Unfortunately, I have been hearing that a lot lately. I

don't know if this helps or not, (That last phrase is so important, it softens the rest), but so many of my customers have told me that it was so much fun to get out of the house and that this party was just what they needed. People aren't traveling, eating out or even going to shopping malls like they did in the past. I think they're getting a little stir crazy. The fact that they can go to a party and purchase something small—or not—and enjoy an evening out with girlfriends is just what they needed. They certainly won't get any pressure from me to purchase anything."

Then close, "What do you think, would you like to schedule a girlfriend night?" Did you notice I said, "I don't know if this helps or not." That is an important part of answering any objection. It lowers resistance because I am saying that I don't know if this is a solution for her, simply a suggestion.

**Objection:** "I don't have time to have a party."
**Response:** "I understand how you feel. I've heard that from so many hostesses lately. I don't know if this is an option, but some of my hostesses have hosted parties at a restaurant or at work during lunchtime or right after work. That way they had a fun time with friends and earned free product without having to take the time to get the house ready or prepare snacks. Would that be something that might work for you?"

**Objection:** "My friends are partied out."
**Response:** "I can certainly understand that! There are so many more direct sales companies than ever before! People are so busy today that they rarely take time for fun or friends. I don't know if this will make a difference, but what if we did your party differently? We could have a Mexican Fiesta theme and serve nachos and margaritas, or we could have a pajama party and all your friends could come in their PJs and sip wine with friends. You would all have a fun girlfriend

evening and it wouldn't be just another party they have to go to! It would be something fun they are looking forward to!"

**Objection:** "I don't know enough people."
**Response:** "That is a challenge, isn't it? I don't know if this makes a difference, but I might be able to help you with that. I'm pretty good at helping my hostesses think of people to invite that they had forgotten about. I could also give ten tickets for a drawing I do at my parties, to every guest who brings two people with her. What do you think? Do you want to give it a try?"

## A Couple of Final Tips

Did you notice when I gave the two dates to choose from that I gave the earlier date last? Would you like Thursday the 28th or Tuesday the 19th? I did that on purpose. People will most often choose the last date they hear, so give them your earliest date last.

Finally, smile when you're on the phone. When you smile, your voice sounds more excited, upbeat and energetic. Try this exercise: Don't smile and try to sound upbeat and energetic and then smile and try to sound monotone or grumpy. You can't do it! When you smile, it will come through to the person on the other end of the phone.

Remember that booking calls can be made year-round, and you can get great results by making calls consistently and by using the short script. See the sample script earlier in this chapter and the Short Script Worksheet below. Give it a try, and you might be surprised at how many parties you book!

## Short Script
(Should take less than 10 minutes)

Introduction:
_____
_____
_____
_____
_____

Permission:
_____
_____

Purpose:
_____
_____
_____
_____

Benefit:
_____
_____
_____
_____

Objection: (Feel, felt, found)
_____
_____
_____

Close:
_____
_____
_____
_____
_____

# 13: BOOKING PARTIES WHEN YOU ARE OUT AND ABOUT

We all know about booking parties at our parties and on the phone. However, how many of us think about booking parties when we are out and about?

My friend Christine shared an example at one of our meetings. She had stood next to a soccer mom several weeks in a row at the games. After several weeks of visiting at the games, she finally stepped way out of her comfort zone and shared her business with this soccer mom. Much to her surprise, Christine booked a party! Christine shared how that party and the parties booked from that and successive parties generated several thousand dollars in sales. In addition to the sales, that one connection resulted in several recruits, and one of those recruits became a leader! All this happened because she stepped out of her comfort zone and asked a casual acquaintance if she'd like to book a party. We never know where one new contact or one new booking can take us.

Someone once said, "When your mouth is closed, so is your business." Of course, the flip side of that is, when your mouth is open, so is your business. Who can we talk to when we're out and about? We can strike up conversations with the people we interact with during our daily routines including sports moms, pre-school parents, classroom parents, church acquaintances, banking acquaintances, coworkers, a favorite grocery clerk, a hairdresser, and even the barista at the coffee stand. Everybody! Even strangers would love your products—if you told strangers about them.

## Opening Up a Dialogue with an Acquaintance

If it's a fellow parent, ask about her child and whether she has other children. Then ask her what she does for a living. When you ask someone what she does, what is the natural thing for her to do? Normally she will answer you and then ask what you do. Unfortunately, many people in direct sales respond in a way that is not very motivating. "Oh well, I have this sort of hobby thing. I do a party here and there, but it's not really my priority." Or "I have this little XYZ business, but it's not working very well for me." Or even, "Oh I kind of sell blah, blah, but not really. I really just signed up to get a discount." Does that sound like someone a person would want to book a party with?

Be ready with a strong and confident thirty-second commercial when someone asks what you do. Be proud! People like to be around people who are sure of themselves and who take pride in their work. Would you rather book a party with someone who is just playing around with their business or someone who is working on and taking pride in their business?

When my business was selling toys and games, I responded with, "I bring families together to have fun and build stronger relationships with each other." People would reply with "Really? How do you do that?" Then we'd have a conversation going and I could share my enthusiasm and passion. I believe that my business built family relationships. I was proud of what I did. I shared my conviction that parents need to spend quantity time with their kids in order to *have* quality time with their kids. I talked about the way kids open up when everyone is sitting around the table playing a game.

When my business was selling candles, I said, "I help people make their homes a more enjoyable place to be." I said that because I meant it! I believe that people enjoy the way their house smells with candles burning, that candles provide a relaxing atmosphere, and that people felt better in homes that were decorated with the beautiful accessories I provided. It wasn't just a sales pitch. I believed what I was saying. Take the time to write your thirty-second commercial. Write one that you believe and feel proud saying. Then when someone asks you what you do, you will have a strong confident answer.

## Opening Up a Conversation with Someone New

It is a good idea to think of ways to continually increase your field of acquaintances. A fun way to meet more people is to wear your nametag when you're out and about. It's a good conversation starter. When you wear your nametag, make sure you are dressed like you're on your way to a party! People won't know whether or not you are on your way to a party, and someone may ask, "Oh, do you sell XYZ? My friend used to sell it." You can then reply, "Oh really? Did she stop selling? Do you need a new consultant?" Or someone could ask, "What does your nametag say? I'm not familiar with that." Your reply could be, "Let me tell you about it." Tell her a little bit about your product and ask "Would you like to have a party?"

Be creative and have some fun with meeting new people. I had a friend who wore her nametag upside down when she was out and about. She said only nice people will say, "Oh dear, your nametag is upside down." With that approach, she only met nice people!

Standing and waiting in a line is a great opportunity to ask someone about her day and what she does. Of course, she will ask you what you do, and you'll have an opportunity to present your thirty-second commercial. It may feel a little uncomfortable at first. Like anything else, the more you do it, the more comfortable it becomes.

Be prepared by keeping catalogs in your purse or car so you always have them handy when you meet someone who is interested. One very important key to remember whenever you give out a catalog is to ask for a phone number so you can follow up. Resist the temptation to say, "My number's on the back. Call me if you'd like to order or book a party." If you tell them to call you, it is very unlikely that they will. Getting a phone number puts you in control of the call.

What else can you do to meet new people and get a conversation going? Wear your brand! Invest in clothing and items that show your company logo and brand. Some items you could consider include shirts, caps, jackets, pens, checkbook covers, purses, tote bags and so on. Whenever there is a contest where you have an opportunity to earn logo items, make sure you earn them! When you are wearing or carrying your company name, people will ask, "Oh you sell XYZ?" or "What is XYZ Company?" Now you have another open door to present your thirty-second commercial and to share what you do. Proudly displaying your product also gives you a tool to invite prospective hostesses to earn free product. Don't tell prospects what you do and leave it hanging there! Make certain you ask if they're interested in earning free product. Ask if they would like to host a party. You never know who will say yes and where that yes will lead you in future business!

# 14: GETTING GREAT RESULTS THROUGH HOSTESS COACHING

Whether you earn $50 or $150 at your parties depends almost entirely on how well you hostess coach! How well you coach your hostess directly impacts how many guests you will have in attendance at your party. The average sale per guest in our business is about $50. If there is one guest at your party, your sales will likely be about $50. If there are ten guests in attendance, your sales will probably be around $500. The goal is to have eight to ten guests in attendance at every party. This is easily attainable with good hostess coaching.

Let's also remember today's woman. Our job is to make hosting a party as easy as possible. We will have fewer cancellations if we do. Remind your hostess at every opportunity how much fun she and her friends and family are going to have at her party, and how they will enjoy a night off.

## Coaching for Success

When is the best time to begin the hostess coaching process? As you begin to hold parties, many of your bookings will come *from* your parties. In that case, do the initial coaching right there that night, especially when you have booked more than one hostess. You can ask the new hostesses if they can take a few minutes before they leave so you can go through their packets with them. Coach all of your new hostesses from the party in a group at one time. This will save you time and it will give you more time to help the other guests at that party. Doing the initial coaching at the party saves you the time of coaching individually over the phone the next day and possibly getting into a phone tag situation. For those parties booked outside of the party—on the phone, through email and so on—the initial coaching will take place a couple of days later when the hostess has received her hostess packet.

Before we actually walk through the initial coaching, I will share with you one of the most common frustrations I have heard from consultants over the years: "I can't get my hostesses to work with me." Consultants coach a hostess on what to do, they follow up, they are excited when they are talking with the hostess, and still the hostess often does not do her part. In most cases, I find that the consultant is doing *almost* everything right. The one piece they are missing is the most important piece. They don't have the hostess's buy-in.

Your hostesses are the key to attendance at your parties. You count on them to personally invite guests and to follow up with a reminder a day or two before the party. However, what do you think the hostess says when we coach them to do that? Many say, "I don't want to be pushy." These are her friends and family. She doesn't want them to feel like she's taking advantage of them. She may even feel guilty about getting free product as a result of what they spend at her party. Consequently, she says, "I'll just send a few emails and we'll see who comes!" This is sure disaster for your party. If we know that's how many hostesses feel, how do we get them to cooperate with us? How do we get them to let us coach them on how to have a successful party?

## Coaching for Hostess Buy-in

One of the most important goals of hostess coaching is to get your hostess's buy-in and partnership. She is the key to your success. It's very hard to get $500 in sales, three bookings, and a new recruit from two guests! I'm going to share with you a proven technique to increase the hostess's buy-in to full cooperation and partnership with you! It just takes a few minutes and makes a big, big difference!

The first thing you will say to your new hostess in the initial contact is something like this:

**You:** "Carli, most of my hostesses have told me that there are three things they want from their party. They want their friends to have fun, to not have their friends feel pressured to buy, and to get some free product for themselves. Does that sound about right Carli?"

Some of the specifics might change with your company. However, the rest of the conversation will go something like this:

**Carli:** "Yes, that sounds right. Actually, my friends having a good time is even more important to me than the free product."
**You:** "Great! I can make sure that all of that happens. I'll just need a little help from you. Carli, I want you to imagine that it is the night of your party, and there are three guests in your living room. The room is kind of quiet, there's not a lot of talking going on, and there's probably not much energy or laughing going on either. Now, imagine that it's the night of your party and there are fifteen people in the room. It's noisy and crazy and everyone is laughing. I can hardly get a word in edgewise! Which group do you think is having more fun?"
**Carli:** "The group of fifteen."
**You:** "Definitely! With fifteen people in attendance, would they feel less pressured to buy than if there were only three?"
**Carli:** Yes, that's probably true."
**You:** "The second group has more fun, they feel less pressured to buy when there is a large group, and you would certainly get more free product!"

## Coaching after Hostess Buy-in

Now that your hostess sees the bigger picture, she will be more receptive to your coaching. It's a quick exercise that takes just a few minutes and makes a big difference in the end result. Next, you will want to go through the hostess packet with her. If you don't go through the packet with her, you will probably find it unopened on the kitchen counter when you arrive to do her party. Include two catalogs and eight guest order forms. If you put in two guest order forms, the subliminal message is that she is supposed to collect two outside orders! If you put in eight forms, she will think she is supposed to collect eight outside orders. Also include a hostess brochure—so she can refer back to it to see what she receives for hosting a party— and a copy of any current hostess or customer specials. Here is an effective way to coach your hostess through her packet:

**You:** "Okay Carli, let's go through your hostess packet. You have two catalogs and eight guest order forms. These are for your outside orders. On average, thirty to fifty percent of the people whom you invite will be unable to attend. You'll want to make sure that those who can't attend have an opportunity to place their orders. Any outside orders you collect count toward your sales. Go ahead and start working on your guest list, and I'll call in a couple of days to see how the list is coming and to help you if needed."

Now you can lead her through the invitation process:

**You:** "For the best attendance, I recommend inviting guests personally and connecting with them several times before the party. A personal invitation can be through face-to-face contact, text, phone, email or Facebook®. A friendly reminder a couple of times before the party will keep it in the forefront of your guests' minds, and a reminder the day before will ensure great attendance and lots of fun and energy at your party. When you invite your friends, family, and coworkers, be sure to talk about how nice it's going to be for *them* to take a break and enjoy a night off as well."

Some consultants send an email invitation to guests as well and that's fine. However, it must not replace any of these personal contacts from the hostess.

Now that you have coached her toward success for her first party, you can get her thinking about the possibility of becoming a consultant herself.

**You:** "There is also some information in your packet about becoming a consultant. It's fun! You can set your own schedule and earn income for the extras that aren't in your budget. There's also a flyer in your packet that shows the customer special we have going on this month. You can share the flyer with your friends that aren't able to make it to your party. We went over the hostess benefits during the party you attended, but let's go over them one more time. It's in your hostess brochure. You get twenty percent of all your sales. For example, if your party sales are $400, then you would receive $80 in free product! You also would get one half-priced item for every $200 in sales. With that same $400 party, you would also be able to choose two half-priced items! That $100 item you love would be a good one to get at half price!"

**Carli:** "Can I use my free product towards my half-priced item?"

**You:** "Great question! It's actually two separate gifts, so you do use them individually. Go ahead and write down everything on your wish list. When we talk next time, I'll help you figure out how much your sales need to be to get everything on your list."

**Carli:** "Okay."

**You:** "Let's talk in a couple of days. How does Wednesday work for you?"

**Carli:** "That works for me."

**You:** "Is two o'clock Okay?"

**Carli:** "Sure."

**You:** "Okay, we'll touch base then."

To recap, on the initial contact with our hostess, we accomplish these goals:

- Get hostess buy-in
- Go through the hostess packet with her
- Encourage her to collect outside orders
- Encourage her to start a guest list and wish list
- Let her know you will do most of the work to ensure she has a successful party
- Briefly offer the business opportunity and go over the hostess plan
- Schedule your next call

### Coaching through the Second Contact

The first thing you will do on the second call is to ask the hostess for her wish list. If she hasn't done that yet, take a few minutes and help her create one. The hostess being clear about what products she wants to earn from her party will help put a sense of urgency on earning those products for free. It will also help you minimize the number of cancelled parties. Once you know what the wish list includes, you can help her figure out how many guests she will need at her party to get it all for free! For instance, if you know that her wish list totaled $100, and she will get twenty percent of her party sales in free product, then she would need a $500 party to earn everything on her wish list for free. An average guest order is about $50, so in order to earn $100 in free product this hostess would need about ten guests in attendance. Typically, thirty to fifty percent of invited guests attend. The hostess would need to invite twenty to thirty people to get the ten that she needs in attendance. Because we are focusing on what's in it for the hostess, she will be willing to let you help her with her guest list.

If the guest list doesn't have thirty names on it yet, offer to help her think of other names. Teach her the F.R.A.N.K. tool from the "Creating a Great Contact List" chapter on page 9. This acronym stands for Friends, Relatives, Acquaintances, Neighbors, and Kid contacts. Ask her to think of two friends who aren't on the list. Then have her consider two relatives that she hasn't included on the list. Now think about two acquaintances, perhaps a hair stylist, nail technician or favorite grocery clerk. Now have her think of two neighbors. Lastly, suggest inviting two people she knows through her children. Maybe it's a soccer mom, a teacher or a Sunday school teacher. That alone will add ten new names to her list. If your hostess still doesn't have thirty names on her guest list, try mixing F.R.A.N.K. up a bit. How about your friend's relatives? Can someone bring her sister or mother? How about your relative's friends? Can your sister bring her friend?

On this second contact, remind your hostess that any outside orders count toward her sales. Remind her to get any outside orders before the party so you can close the party out that night. This is a huge time saver for you. When you leave that night, all you have to do is submit the party or put in your order. Your customers will get their product faster if the hostess doesn't need several days to wrap up her outside orders.

Be sure to encourage your hostess to keep her refreshments simple. It's easier for her, and you are more likely to book more parties at her party if it looks easy and fun to be a hostess. Lastly, remind her again of what she earns for hosting a party. Make sure that you are smiling and excited. Even over the phone, your smile will come through in your voice.

Here is an example of how that second phone conversation might sound:

**You:** "Hi Carli, it's Shari with XYZ company. We had an appointment to talk today at 2. Is this still a good time?"

**Carli:** "Yes! This is fine!"

**You:** "Good! I'm anxious to hear what's on your wish list, Carli!"

**Carli:** "Well, I haven't really thought about it yet."

**You:** "That's okay. We can do that together. It will only take a few minutes. Do you have your catalog handy?"

**Carli::** "It's here somewhere…oh here it is."

**You:** "I have mine too. We'll go through it together, and I'll write down the items you want to earn."

Create the wish list together. Now you can use her wish list to coach her through her guest list.

**You:** "Okay! Let's add this up! Carli, your wish list totals $115. You receive twenty percent of your sales in free product and one half-price item for every $200 in sales. You will need a $570 party to get everything on your wish list for free, plus you will still get to choose two half-priced items! Our average party guest order is $50, so eleven or twelve orders will get you your $570 party. That could be accomplished with ten guests at your party and a couple of outside orders! Now, remember that thirty to fifty percent of those you invite will attend, so you will need a guest list of twenty to thirty people. How is your guest list coming along?"

**Carli:** "Pretty good! I have ten names so far."

**You:** "That's great! Would you like some help getting that up to twenty or thirty?"

**Carli:** "Okay. I'm not sure how you can help me think of people for my guest list, but I'm game!"

**You:** "It's just a little mind jogger exercise, but it really works. Do you already have some friends on your list?"

**Carli:** "I do! I have four!"

**You:** "Great! Can you add two more friends? They don't have to be your best friends, just friends."

**Carli:** "Okay, Ellen and Carmen."

**You:** "Now how about two relatives? Your sister, cousin, mother, aunt, brother, sister-in-law?"

**Carli:** "Oh, I didn't think about in-laws! There's Mary, Vicki, John, . . . oh . . . and Cindy, my husband's niece!"

**You:** "Wow! Great! Now let's add two acquaintances: your hair stylist, your nail tech, your favorite barista, a coworker . . . people you wouldn't necessarily have over to dinner, but they're people you know and see on a regular basis."

**Carli:** "My nail gal Monica, and Erin from my women's group! Oh, and Beth and Kathryn from work."

**You:** "You're doing great! How about two neighbors?"

**Carli:** "We live on ten acres and don't really know the neighbors very well."

**You:** "That's okay! How about two people you know through your children? A soccer mom, a PTA parent, or a youth group parent?"

**Carli:** "Oh, my gosh! I bet Sylvia and Janey would love to come! I see them every Saturday at gymnastics."

**You:** "Wow Carli! You just added twelve names! You're up to twenty-two! Should we see if we could get to thirty?"

**Carli:** "Sure! Why not?"

**You:** "Okay! How about a relative's friend? Could your mom bring a friend? How about your sister's friends or coworkers?"

**Carli:** "I'll ask my mom to bring Ella, and I'll see if my sister-in-law wants to bring her friend Jen, and I'll ask my sister to bring her best friends Sarah and Celeste."

**You:** "Four more to go! How about your friends' relatives?"

**Carli:** "Oh, I love Libby's mom! I'll tell her to bring her. She is awesome and Amber's really close to her sister. She'd probably love to bring her!"

**You:** "How about friends' acquaintances, coworkers, a church friend?"

**Carli:** "You know, Barb does a lot of things with her friends from work. I'll ask her to bring two of them!"

**You:** "Congratulations! You have thirty names on your list!"

**Carli:** "Thanks Shari, I wouldn't have thought of those guys without your help!"

**You:** "You did awesome, Carli. I have a few more things to cover with you. Remember, the first invitation will come from you. You'll want to invite your guests personally, either face to face, over the phone, through text, email or Facebook®. I know it's quicker and easier to send out a group invitation. However, let me ask you to consider these two approaches: You receive a group email from a friend that says, 'I'm having a home décor party on Thursday the 28th at 7:00 at my house! Hope you can all come!' Or you get a personal phone call from a friend who says, 'Hey Carli! I'm having a home décor party on Thursday the 28th at seven o'clock at my house. They have really beautiful products. I know you'll love it! I called you as soon as I booked it so you could put it on your calendar! It's always more fun when you're there! Can you make it?' Which one would you be more likely to respond positively to? Which made you feel more special?"

**Carli:** "Definitively the personal invitation!"

**You:** "Good! Once you've personally invited all your guests, please send me the names and email addresses of the confirmed guests. I'll send out an e-invite right away. Don't forget to give anyone who can't attend a chance to order. Outside orders count toward your total sales. Please collect any outside orders before your party. I close my parties the night of the party so the guests get their orders right away. Carli, please keep refreshments simple, like cookies with coffee or chips and salsa with wine. Make it easy for yourself, and have one less thing to stress about."

**Carli:** "I was thinking wine and cheese?"

**You:** "Perfect! Do you have any questions for me?"

**Carli:** "No, I don't think so. I'm getting excited! This is going to be fun!"

**You:** "It is going to be so much fun for you and your friends! You're a great hostess! You've been awesome to work with Carli! I'll check in with you the day before your party and get directions. Is two o'clock still a good time?"

**Carli:** "Yes! That's a good time for me!"

**You:** "Okay, I'll talk to you then! Bye."

**Carli:** "Bye, Shari."

To recap, on the second contact you want to accomplish these goals:

• Go over hostess wish list
• Remind her what she will receive for hosting the party
• Help her create her guest list
• Remind her that the initial invitation needs to come from her
• Encourage her to keep refreshments simple

## Coaching through the Third Contact

The third hostess coaching contact will take place the day before the party. Ask your hostess how her outside orders are going. Remind her to get all outside orders in before the party. Find out how many guests she is expecting by asking how many guest folders you should bring. It feels more like you want to be prepared for her guests, rather than being concerned there might not be enough people there. Encourage your hostess to remind her guests about her party. A hostess is sometimes hesitant to do this. She doesn't want her friends to feel she is pestering them.

During this call, you will get directions and confirm with your hostess what time you will arrive before the party. Then, be on time. Being a few minutes early may not seem like a big deal to us, but often your hostess is not ready even a few minutes early. If I arrived early, I parked a block away and made booking or hostess coaching calls.

Here is an example of how the third contact might sound:

**You:** "Hi Carli, it's Shari. Is this still a good time for you?"

**Carli:** "I'm just folding clothes, this is fine."

**You:** Thank you for getting me your guest list and email addresses so quickly. I sent out all the e-invites. Did you get yours?"

**Carli:** "Yes, I did!"

**You:** "Oh good! How are your outside orders coming?"

**Carli:** "Great! I have five!"

**You:** "That's awesome! Have you added them up?"

**Carli:** "It's about $200!"

**You:** "Wow Carli! You're a great salesperson! You might want to think about doing this."

**Carli:** "Me? I don't have the right personality for this kind of thing."

**You:** "What do you mean?"

**Carli:** "Well, I'm not very outgoing. I'm kind of shy, actually."

**You:** "I think most people feel that way. I know I felt really nervous about talking to people I didn't know. Like I did, you would start with friends and family. Then you'll meet new people at their parties and book parties with them. I think it is easier to do parties for strangers than friends and family. I didn't worry as much about what they thought or how I was doing, and I actually got better and more comfortable after a few parties. I hope you'll think about it! Carli, you'll want to contact your guests today and remind them of your party tomorrow."

**Carli:** "I think they'll remember, and I don't want to bug them."

**You:** "I understand that, but one last reminder will really make a difference in your attendance! What if you just say something like, 'Hi Mom, I'm getting my snacks ready for tomorrow and I want to have plenty! Are you bringing your friend?' You're actually reminding them of the party and to bring a friend!"

**Carli:** "Oh, I like that. That sounds better than 'don't forget.'"

**You:** "I want to make sure I bring enough guest folders. How many confirmed guests do you have so far?"

**Carli:** "Twelve have said they'll be here. If that changes after I make my calls today, I'll let you know!"

**You:** "That's sounds great, Carli. Your party is at seven o'clock so I'll be there at 6:40 to set up and be ready to meet your friends!"
**Carli:** "Great, I'll see you then!"

To recap, on the third contact, you want to accomplish these goals:
• Ask the hostess about her outside orders
• Congratulate her on getting the outside orders
• Coach her to remind her guests about the party
• Confirm the number of guests attending
• Tell her what time you'll arrive

## Successful Coaching Accomplished

That's it! Just a few phone calls coaching your hostess will make all the difference in the success of her party! That means more products for her and more income, bookings, and recruits for you.

## Keep an Eye on the Time You Invest

There is one last thing I want to make sure we cover. You probably noticed that all of these contacts were over the phone, except for the initial coaching done with hostesses booked at a party. I've heard leaders and consultants talk over the years about the success they have doing their hostess coaching in person. They talk about the rapport and relationship being stronger and their sales being higher at the parties where they have done face-to-face coaching.

While that may be true, I strongly discourage this practice. First of all, it is not an effective use of your time. It may be manageable for a consultant holding one or two parties a month. However, even at that, with driving time to her house or even a coffee shop, it is probably going to be over an hour per contact, probably closer to an hour and a half. By the time you've met your hostess three times to get through the three coaching contacts, you have three to four-and-a-half hours into coaching. Add that to actual party time and you are at five to six hours per party. If you spend forty-five minutes total on three contacts over the phone and add in party time, you are at two to two-and-a-half hours per party. That's a lot more money per hour in your pocket!

Think about how this practice could impact your bookings. If a consultant told me I needed to meet with her three times before my party, I wouldn't book! Would you? You and your hostesses lead full, busy lives. You want to make this easy for them and you! Be conscious of your ROTI: Return on Time Invested! Work smarter, not harder.

# Three Contact Hostess Coaching

## First coaching contact

Ask if this is still a good time to talk

1. Get buy-in from hostess - help her understand how her efforts can make a difference in the success of her party
2. Go through the hostess packet with her
   - Hostess brochure
   - Guest order forms and catalogs for outside orders
   - Copy of any current hostess or customer specials
   - Recruiting brochure
3. Coach her to:
   - Collect outside orders before night of the party
   - Start working on a guest list
   - Make a "wish list"
4. Schedule time to call back within 48 hours

## Second coaching contact
Ask if this is still a good time to talk

1. Smile, be enthusiastic
2. Go over "wish list" (or create one together)
3. Calculate amount of sales needed to earn the "wish list"
4. Help her create guest list using F.R.A.N.K.
5. Coach her to personally invite guests
6. Ask her to send you her guest list with addresses and email addresses
7. Coach her to keep refreshments simple
8. Remind her to get all outside orders before the night of the party
9. Briefly offer the opportunity to join your team

## Third coaching contact
Ask if this is still a good time to talk

1. Ask her how her outside orders are coming
2. Share how to make reminder calls to her guests
3. Ask her how many guest folders you will need
4. Get directions
5. Tell her what time you'll arrive

# 15: DEVELOPING A RECRUITING MINDSET

Recruiting is your path to a six-figure income. Not only will recruiting bring you financial rewards, it's also the most rewarding part of this business in so many other ways.

Once you start recruiting and seeing your new recruits' success, you will feel an intense sense of pride and a new excitement for the business. It will quickly become your favorite part of your business.

## Change Your Mental Picture

So what stops us from recruiting? Our perceptions. Recruiting is easy when you change the way you think about it. A common perception about recruiting is that you have to be pushy. Let me put your mind at ease. Being pushy is not effective. In fact, it doesn't work at all. People resist—and resent—pushy people.

Here are four thoughts that really helped me change my perception about recruiting:

1. "You can get anything you want out of life if you just help enough other people get what they want." —Zig Ziglar, Self-help author and speaker.

2. Recruiting is simply sharing something you believe in with someone who will benefit from it. When you recruit someone into

the business, you both win. Do you believe in what you're doing? Have you and your family benefited from your business? Are you happier? Has your business relieved some financial pressure? Have you grown personally as a result of your business? Are there others who would enjoy or need those same benefits?

3. Focus on your prospect. If we can forget about the benefit to us, and really focus on the benefit to others, it's so much easier for us to recruit. Sometimes, just the idea that we get something for recruiting hinders us. When we are totally focused on our prospect, it's mentally much easier for us to recruit. That means thinking about how your business could benefit them. Do they need extra money? Do they need to get out of the house a couple of nights a week? Do they love to be center stage? Are they naturally inclined to help people? If you're nervous or afraid to ask, you're focused on the wrong person. Focus on them, and it will be much easier to recruit.

4. Our job is to offer. Their job is to accept or decline. If we don't offer, we've ultimately made the decision for them. I've heard consultants over the years say things like: "I didn't ask her because she has three young children." "She makes too much money, she wouldn't be interested." "She's too old." "She's too young." "She's too busy." "She's too shy." We need to let them decide if it is a good choice for their life, not decide for them.

### You Never Know Who Is Ready to Join You

When I was a corporate trainer, one of our top-level leaders was a mortgage broker with a six-figure income when someone shared our company's business opportunity with her and she said yes. Her reason for agreeing was that she was working eighty hours a week as a mortgage broker. She replaced that income quickly and quit the mortgage business.

Another leader was a district attorney who just needed "something fun in her life." One of the ladies on my team was working a full -time job and five part-time jobs when she joined my team. As her income grew, she quit the jobs one by one. Today she is one of the top income earners in her company. Another woman joined my team for the sole purpose of overcoming her shyness.

We never know what our business opportunity can do for someone else. With that said, we can certainly make our offer in a way that makes it appealing, in a way that is more likely to get a "yes." Let me show you what I mean.

## Make Your Offer Compelling

Imagine you and your family are out to dinner. You've finished your meal and the server comes by, offers you more coffee and asks if you'd care for any dessert. How likely are you to say, "Yes, I'd love some dessert. What do you have?" Not very likely!

Now imagine that as you finish your meal, your server comes by, offers you coffee and says, "Let me tell you about a few of our dessert offerings. We have the best cheesecake in the state. We drizzle a wonderful raspberry puree over it, and then we top it with a touch of whipped cream. Or perhaps you're a chocolate fan. You'll love our chocolate fudge cake. We pour hot fudge over the top and serve it with a scoop of vanilla ice cream. Then there's my personal favorite, our famous apple crisp, with a great crumbled topping and served warm. What do you think? May I bring you a dessert menu, or did I tempt you with one of our specialties?"

Isn't it more tempting to say yes to the second offer? The server painted a picture—he helped us visualize. We could almost taste it. It's the same with recruiting. We don't have to be pushy. Our job is to make the offer; theirs is to accept or decline. However, like the server, we can learn to make our offer in a way that is more appealing, in a way that makes people want to say, "Yes!" You'll find suggestions throughout the next chapter to make what you're offering very desirable.

## Embrace Hearing No

A big thing that keeps people from recruiting is the fear of hearing no. I once heard someone say, "We would all be successful if it weren't for the fear of rejection." We think when someone says no to us that they are rejecting us. That's not true.

What if you were at a friend's house, and she offered you and her other guests a brownie. Some of the guests said yes, but you said, "No, thank you. I'm on a diet." Were you rejecting her? Of course not. You were just trying to stick to your diet. Others did say yes though, and maybe on another day you would too.

Recruiting is the same. You may offer several people the business opportunity and some will say yes and others will say, "No, thank you." Even though some said no this time, it doesn't mean they won't say yes later. Circumstances change. I asked one of my top leaders to become a consultant five times before she said yes. Today, she earns a six-figure income. We are both glad I kept asking.

When you change the way you think about recruiting, you will change the way you ask, and then you will change your results.

# 16: THE VERY BEST PLACE TO RECRUIT IS AT YOUR PARTIES

There is someone at every party who wants to join your business—they just don't know it yet. The key is to make sure that you go into every party with a recruiting focus. Most of us tend to go into our parties with a sales focus, a hope for bookings and a low focus on recruiting.

At a party, you have the entire duration of the event to build excitement and desire around joining your team. How do you make sure you don't miss someone who would benefit from your business opportunity?

One of the best ways to maximize your recruiting success at a party is through excellent hostess coaching. Effective hostess coaching equals high attendance, which equals high sales. We do that before the party, so we don't need to focus on sales at the party. With eight to ten guests who place an average order of $50, your party should produce sales of $400 to $500.

Another smart technique is to play a booking game and place effective booking seeds throughout your presentation. With eight to ten guests at your party, you can easily book two or more new parties.

This allows you to go into your parties with one antenna—your recruiting antenna. By just focusing on recruiting, you'll notice:

- Someone whose eyes get big when you talk about the income opportunity.
- Someone who's crazy about the product.
- Someone who gets excited when you talk about the incentive trip. You will hear clues like: "I love to travel." "We could use a second car." "It's so great to have a break from my toddlers." "I had so much fun tonight."

Use your recruiting antenna to pick up on these comments. Potential recruits are telling you how your business could benefit them.

### Three Ways to Respond to the Same Comment

Think about how you might respond to this comment if you had a sales focus at your party:

"I'd love to get that XYZ product, but it's a little out of my budget." You might think, "That's an expensive piece. I need that sale!" and you would immediately begin to tell her all the benefits of that product.

If you went into the party with a booking focus, and you heard the same comment you might think, "She should book a party and get it for free." You would share with her how she could earn that incredible piece for free by hosting her own party.

If you went into the party with a recruiting focus and heard the same comment, you might think, "If it's out of her budget, she might be able to use some extra income." You could say something like, "I don't know if this is anything you would be interested in, but I'd love to share with you a fun way to increase your monthly income. Would you like to take home some information?"

Depending on our focus, we will hear and respond differently to customer comments. The first key to being a consistent recruiter is to go into your parties with one antenna—your recruiting antenna.

Secondly, building rapport with your guests can have a big impact on recruiting at your parties. You can begin to build rapport with guests the moment they arrive. I always offered to be the greeter so the hostess could be free to take care of last minute details. You can greet the guest, introduce yourself and ask her name. You'll want to use nametags at your parties, so you can call them by name throughout the evening. People like to be called by their name. Ask them questions. People love to talk about themselves. I once talked to a gentleman on an airplane for several hours. I asked him questions the entire flight. By then end of the flight, I knew his life story. He knew nothing about me, including my name. He did tell me it was the most interesting conversation he'd had in years!

You can ask your guests things like: Are you coming from work? How was the traffic? How is that commute? Do you have children? How do you know the hostess? By taking the time to get to know the guests a little bit and showing genuine interest in them, you'll find they respond to you more warmly during your presentation. Not only does asking questions help build rapport, you can also learn a lot about someone in a short period of time.

They will give you clues as to why your business might benefit them! They might say, "I'm actually coming from home, I've been looking forward to this all day! I love being a stay-at-home mom, but it's sure nice to get out once in a while!" She just told you it would be nice to get out of the house once in a while. Could you help her with that? She might say, "I came from work." "Where do you work?" "I'm an attorney." "Wow, I'll bet that's rewarding work!" "You know I love it, but it can be a pretty negative environment sometimes."

She just told you that she could use a positive outlet occasionally. Can you help her with that? Before the party starts, sit with the guests and interact with them. Don't monopolize the conversation, just be a part of it. During the party, you can continue to build rapport by calling people by name, asking for their opinion, smiling, and saying things like "That's a great idea!" "You're very creative." "I've never thought of that." The simple act of paying people genuine compliments in front of others is a strong rapport builder. During the shopping period, stay in the room with your guests. I've seen so many consultants pick up their calculator and go into the kitchen to wait for the orders. By staying in the room with the guests and approaching each guest to see if they need help finding anything and being accessible for questions, you are actually continuing to build rapport while at the same time giving good customer service.

Remember that shopping time is "code" for visiting time! When you're in the room with the guests, you get to hear their conversations. When Susie tells Mary that John just got laid off and she's totally stressed about money, you hear that! You're building rapport and gathering information that will help you recruit. Here's a quick tip to help build rapport during the shopping period. Kneel down when you are helping a customer. The guests are generally sitting on a couch or in a chair. When you stand, they have to look up at you and you are looking down on them. It's similar to someone interviewing a job candidate, and having that person sit in the shorter chair and look up at the person interviewing. It's intimidating! Looking down at your customer can send a subliminal negative message. Looking up to the customer sends a subliminal positive message and creates a warmer atmosphere.

## Plant Recruiting Seeds

Seeds are not direct thought provokers like, "Watch what I do tonight and see how easy it is." Those are good too. A recruiting seed is so subtle they don't even know they heard it.

A recruiting seed might sound like this: "I'm going to give you ladies an extra ticket for the drawing tonight because you're so fun! I love getting out and visiting with great women a couple of times a week, but you are an extra fun group." Consciously they hear that they were an "extra fun group." The hidden seed is that you get out a couple of times a week.

Another recruiting seed might be, "This is one of my favorite products. It came in my first kit five years ago and I still bring it to every party."

They consciously hear that that product is one of your favorites, but the subtle seed is that you get a kit as a consultant, with lots of fun things in it.

A recruiting seed can be as simple as having a picture of you and your husband on the incentive trip in your display, or it could be a picture of you and your friends at your national conference. It could be a picture of anything your business has paid for, like your daughter at her gymnastics class. Of course, someone will ask about the picture, giving you a built-in opportunity to share one of the ways your business has helped you or your family.

You'll want to plant seeds that communicate the following:
• It's fun
• It's profitable
• It's flexible
• It's rewarding

Seeds build desire, but they need to be scripted and practiced. You don't want to count on them just popping into your head during your presentation. Use the template at the end of this chapter to create your own booking seeds.

## Pre-Plan Your Personal Commercial

Sharing your personal commercial midway through your party is a great way to create a desire to become a consultant. Make it short—about sixty seconds or less—and share four key messages.

1. Why you started the business originally (It has probably changed since then—just share one reason)

2. What you were nervous about before you started

3. How your life is better today because of your business

4. What you love most about your business today

When we talk about only one aspect, there may be only one person in the room who will relate. For instance if you said, "I got started in this business to get out of the house once a week," there may be only one person in the room who resonates with that message. By speaking to four different aspects, most people in the room can relate to at least one of them.

Your commercial could sound like this: "I got started with (your company) to earn enough money to buy new living room furniture. I was so nervous that I wouldn't get any bookings. I was surprised that I earned enough money in two months to buy the furniture and still had eight more bookings! That was a year ago. Thanks to my business, we have lots of little extras we didn't have before, like a debt-free Christmas and long weekend vacations, and I can treat myself to things like a pedicure without feeling guilty. I think my favorite part is all the new friends I've made: my hostesses and customers, and the other consultants who really helped me to learn how to do this."

## Play the Question Game

Follow your personal commercial with a short question/answer period. You could give raffle tickets for a small prize if they ask you a question. A question and answer time works well because you aren't standing up front in lecture mode telling them everything you love about your business. They are asking questions and you are simply answering them. It's an easier way for them to take in the information.

However, if you just say, "Okay, this is your opportunity to ask me anything about my business," you'll have a long, uncomfortable silence. You have to give them starter questions to get the conversation going, and then they will get so involved that you'll have to stop or it will go on forever!

To get it started, you can say something like this: "Okay! It's question time. This is your opportunity to ask me anything you want to about my business. It has to be about my business. You can't ask how old I am, but you can ask me about our incentive trip to Hawaii, our $1000 bonus, how much I earn, or how much you could earn holding a couple of parties a week. For every question you ask, I will give you a ticket, and at the end of the question and answer period, we'll draw for a prize. Who wants to go first?"

Of course, the starter questions are the first ones they ask, so make sure they are the questions you want them to ask. At the end of your question and answer time, wrap it up with a group offer to join the business.

A group offer could sound like this: "I hope this question and answer time gave some of you food for thought. You can try the business for a few weeks and see what you think. There's really nothing to lose. If you like it, you'll have a great business going. If you don't, you can quit. It's really that simple. The worst thing that can happen is that you will have earned some extra money and gotten a lot of great products in your kit."

When my team started using that verbiage, our recruiting went up seventy percent in one month and our team sales doubled the next month. Words like "career" or "start a business" can make people nervous. They sound like a long-term commitment or that there's a big investment. "Try it for three weeks," says it is on a trial basis. The bottom line is that signing up means they are going to try it for a short time and see if they like it. You just made it easier to say yes.

Apply the ideas in this chapter and watch your recruiting flourish. Then share these ideas with your team and watch everyone flourish. Ongoing recruiting is the key to building a successful team.

# 17: RECRUITING: HOW TO APPROACH, FOLLOW UP AND HANDLE OBJECTIONS

When looking for people to join you in your business, the most likely person to say yes is your hostess. You can start talking to her about the opportunity when you start the hostess coaching process. As you go through her hostess packet with her, point out the recruiting brochure and say something simple like, "Mary, I've included a brochure on the business opportunity. I always put one in my hostess packets because so many hostesses are interested. This business is fun, flexible and gives you money for those little extras that aren't in the budget."

On the second contact, casually mention it again. "Mary, I'm really enjoying working with you, I hope you're thinking about giving this business a try. It could be a great way for you to earn a little extra income."

When you get to the party to set up, you can say "Mary, watch what I do tonight and see how easy it is!"

One of the reasons you ask your hostess to get her outside orders before you arrive is so that you can say something like this at the end of her party: "Mary, with your outside orders your total sales were $520. That's awesome! You did a great job! Do you know that if you were the consultant at this party, you would have earned an additional $156? The way you love to fuss over people, you would be a terrific consultant. By the way, you got three bookings tonight that I'll give to you. What do you think? Do you want to try it for a few weeks and see what you think?"

Even if the hostess says no, what do you think she does? She tells all her friends at the party how much money you made that night and that will help you recruit the guests.

Remember, surveys tell us that one out of four hostesses would say yes if you ask them. Let's go back to the last thing I said to the hostess. "You got three bookings that I'll give to you." It is much more tempting for your hostess to say yes when you're handing her three bookings! Remember that a new recruit holding future parties that you are paid commissions on as a leader is always better than the commissions and bookings from just one party!

Susie is a great example of this. She was one of my hostesses. Her party totaled $1,800 and we got six bookings that night. I recruited her and gave up my commission and six bookings. Susie was my top seller until I left that company. She became a leader, earned the incentive trips, and to this day is one of my dearest friends. What was more profitable, the $684 I would have made on her party and the bookings from her party or the tens of thousands of dollars I earned on Susie and her downline over the years?

You want to offer the opportunity to the hostess by sharing what she could have earned (not what you earned), tell her why she'd be good, and then ask if she'd like to try it for a few weeks and see what she thinks.

Keep in mind that "Try it for a few weeks" is a lot less intimidating than "Would you like to join my team?" or "Would you be interested in starting your own business?"

## Approaching Guests at Your Parties

Listen and watch for their hot buttons (the "why they should") and the reason they would be good (the "why they could"). Here are some samples of how that could sound:

1. "Jeanine, I noticed that you're really professional. People like you make great consultants! It would give you an opportunity to earn extra money for the new furniture you mentioned. Would you like to try it for a few weeks and see what you think?"

2. "Michelle, I was noticing that you really like to help people. You were helping Cindy find things in the catalog and helping the hostess clean up the kitchen. People are drawn to you and your kindness. I think you'd make an excellent consultant. It would give you an opportunity to get out of the house once or twice a week. Would you like to try it for a few weeks and see what you think?"

3. "Tina, you were the funniest person here tonight! People love to be around you. Would you consider trying this for a few weeks and see what you think? I could see you being recognized at meetings as a superstar with *your* personality. "

When you offer the opportunity with a compliment to someone, it's not unusual for her friends sitting around her to say, "You are fun! You should try it! You are professional and you're so organized! You'd be great at this!" Her friends will actually help you recruit her.

The important thing is to offer the opportunity—even if all you can remember to say is "Would you be interested in trying this for a few weeks to see what you think?"

Remember that courage is being afraid and doing it anyway. Be courageous in your recruiting approach and you might be amazed at the results you get!

### Follow-Up Is the Key to Everything

Always follow up within 24 to 48 hours. This is so important. After the first 24-48 hours, your prospects will not be nearly as excited.

Here's a sample follow-up script:

**Shari:** "Hi Susan, it's Shari with XYZ. We had an appointment to talk today at one o'clock. Is this still a good time?"
**Susan:** "Yes, this is great!"
**Shari:** "Good! Did you have a chance to look over the information I sent home with you?:"
**Susan:** "I did. I looked at it when I got home last night."
**Shari:** "Great! Were you thinking about going to Hawaii for free today?"
**Susan:** "Oh, that would be great, but I'm sure that's a lot of work, and I don't have a lot of extra time."
**Shari:** "Most people think that. I can see why you might think that, if it's a free trip to Hawaii, it must be really hard! Let me ask you, Susan, if you were to do this, how many parties do you imagine you would have to do each week to earn a trip to Hawaii?"
**Susan:** "I don't know—maybe four or five?"
**Shari:** "If I told you that if you did two parties a week, and that would be about five hours of your time, would you be interested in hearing more?"
**Susan:** "You're kidding! Sure!"
**Shari:** "That's really all it takes and I can help you map out a plan to get there. You'll love the trip! It's a trip for two, and the company pays for everything—your airfare, your hotel and your meals. There's a special banquet on the last night. The best part for me is just lying around the pool all day with my husband and relaxing. We

look forward to the trip every year. We'd never take a trip like that otherwise, and certainly not without the kids. Along the way, you'll probably earn about $200 a week. What would you do with an extra $800 a month?"

**Susan:** "I'd put it away for the trip!"

**Shari:** "That's a great idea! So, do you want to give it a try for a few weeks and see how it feels? What have you got to lose?"

**Susan:** "I guess so, why not!"

If your prospective consultant hasn't looked at the information, it might sound like this:

**Shari:** "Hi Amber, it's Shari with the XYZ Company. We were going to talk at three o'clock today. Is this still a good time?"

**Amber:** "Sure, I have a few minutes."

**Shari:** "Did you have a chance to look over the information I sent home with you?"

**Amber:** "You know I didn't. It's been crazy."

**Shari:** "That's okay. Is it close by?"

**Amber:** "Yes it's here in my purse."

**Shari:** "Why don't you pull it out and we'll just look at the part I think will interest you the most together. You can look over the rest later.

**Amber:** Okay, I've got it."

**Shari:** "Good. Open it up and look on the right side. There's a simple chart that shows you what you can earn holding one party a week, two parties a week and three parties a week. You can figure about two hours of your time from the time you arrive until the time you leave for each party. What number of parties per week do you think would fit best in your life?"

**Amber:** "I could probably fit in two."

**Shari:** "Okay. Great! That means you would earn about $800 a month. I know you wanted to enroll your daughter in gymnastics. Would that cover it?"

**Amber:** "Oh, yes and then some. There would be about $500 left over."

**Shari:** "Wow! What would you do with that?"

**Amber:** "I don't know. We've never had anything left over!"

**Shari:** "Well, would that relieve some of the financial pressure? Could you treat yourself to some of those little extras? How about doing some fun things? Or would you save for a vacation? Christmas? What do you think you would do with that extra money?"

**Amber:** "You know, I think I'd save for a vacation!"

**Shari:** "That's a fun idea. Do you want to try it for a few weeks and see what you think?"

## Overcoming the Top Three Recruiting Objections

Overcoming objections with prospective recruits is where many consultants get stuck. They offer, they follow up, but as soon as they get an objection, they freeze. They don't know what to say, or they don't want to be pushy. Instead, they say, "Okay, thank you for your time," and hang up. What most people don't understand is that an objection is often just a concern or a request for more information.

Your prospect might be thinking, "It might be fun to do this, but how would I fit it into my very busy life?" What she might say is "I'm just too busy." How many of us have immediately given up and said, "Okay, I understand."? Instead, offer a solution and you have a good chance of recruiting that person.

A great way to offer a solution is with the *feel, felt, found* technique like we talked about in the chapter, "Making an Effective Booking Call." When you go right to the solution with, "You know this business is flexible and you can work it around your schedule," it can feel like you're not listening to your prospect. Even worse, it might feel like you are arguing with her, and you won't get the response you're looking for. When you move right into solution mode, you might actually see your prospect tense up. When you use the *feel, felt, found* technique, you are validating her concern by saying, "I can certainly understand how you feel." You are relating to her when you say, "I felt that way when someone shared the opportunity with me," and then you can offer a solution.

However, remember that it's a very old and well-used technique and many people are familiar with it. So let's just change the wording a little. You'll notice below that I use the following language: "I don't know if this helps or not, but . . . " That phrase says I'm not assuming this will work. It's just a suggestion and it breaks down her resistance to the solution.

Also, when someone gives you an objection, pause and nod your head. This tells them you are listening to them, that you genuinely hear their concern. You'll want to purposely slow down your speech and soften your tone. It will make them more receptive to your response.

Here are the three most common recruiting objections and how to respond to them:

**Objection:** "I'm just too busy."
**Response:** "I can certainly understand why you would feel that way. So many people I talk to these days are so busy. It can be daunting to think about adding something else to your already hectic schedule. I don't know if this will make a difference, but what I've heard from other consultants who work full-time or have many commitments is that earning $100 at a party was so appealing that they decided to cut out TV for one night a week to schedule a party. Or they scheduled two parties on Saturday, two weekends a month, so they were only working their business two days a month, and adding $400 to their monthly household income at the same time! What do you think? Would you like to try it for a few weeks and see how it fits in your schedule?"

**Objection:** "I could never stand up in front of people and talk like you do."

**Response:** "You are in good company if that's what makes you nervous! It is the majority of people's number one fear. I know I was very nervous. I don't know if this helps or not, but I found that with each party I did, it got easier. You know what? Now I don't get nervous at all. In fact, it has really helped my confidence and I have overcome that fear. You could even sit on the floor and give your presentation if it makes you feel more comfortable. What do you think? Would you like to try it for a few weeks and see if you feel comfortable?"

**Objection:** "I can't afford to invest in a kit."

**Response:** "I know it's hard to think about spending money to make money. I don't know if this helps or not, but I was surprised to find that I could get started for as little as $125. I realized that I could have my kit in about a week, and I could start holding parties right away. If you held four parties in your first month, you would not only pay for your kit, but you would earn another $275 on top of that. How does that sound? Would you like to try it for a few weeks and see how much you can earn?"

Remember, when you get an objection,
- Validate it. "I understand."
- Relate to it. "I found that myself."
- Then offer a solution.

Successful recruiting is really as simple as approaching people in a genuine way, following up in a timely manner and handling their objections with confidence so that they find it easy to say yes!

Take some time to practice the above steps, and at your next party, know that there is a good chance you will recruit your hostess, or maybe one of the guests!

# 18: BOOKING PARTIES AT PARTIES

When thinking about how to book parties at parties, remember the top three reasons people book parties today:

1. To have fun
2. To earn free product
3. To help a friend

Your parties are absolutely the best place to book parties! You have the entire duration of your party presentation to build excitement for holding a party, to show them how much fun a party is, how much free product they can earn and how they can help their friend, the hostess, by booking a party!

## Leave Any Frustrations from Home at Home

Before we discuss different tools and strategies for maximizing your bookings at your parties, it is important to note that your guests must see you having fun. If there were any crisis, challenges or arguments going on in your life that day, don't take them with you to the party. When you get in your car to drive to the party and close the car door, also close the door on any issues at home! Leave them there. They'll still be there when you get home. Meanwhile, give yourself a couple of hours of relief and fun. For example don't tell your guests that your basement flooded when the washing machine overflowed and ruined the carpet in the family room. That will definitely affect the fun element of your party!

## Great Beginnings Ensure Success

How can you ensure that your parties are fun for the hostess and her guests? From the minute the guests begin to arrive, you can make them feel comfortable, relaxed and special. Greet each guest right away and give her a nametag. They'll actually forget they are wearing nametags, and people love to be called by their names. It's a natural rapport builder. You can continue to build rapport by asking them questions that show genuine interest, like:

• How do you know the hostess?
• Do you have children? How old are they?
• Are you coming from work or home?

People appreciate that you are interested in them, and people love to talk about themselves and their family. It's fun for them!

## Interaction Makes a Big Difference

You can make the party fun for your guests by doing an interactive event, one that involves the guests and the hostess. They will have a lot more fun if they are participating, rather than listening to you in lecture mode for thirty minutes.

An interactive party can be as simple as holding up a product and giving away raffle tickets in return for suggestions from the guests on what to do with the product. You can give tickets to someone who owns that particular product and is willing to share what she loves about it. You can ask questions like, "Who knows what our hostesses get for having a party?" Involving them in the presentation keeps their attention and makes it fun for them.

Another strategy to use is the *gift bag party*. Take ten gift bags and put one piece of product in each bag. Also put one item that is a clue to something you want to talk about during your presentation. You might put a heart in one bag to remind you to talk about your hostess being the heart of your business; $100 play money in another to remind you to talk about the opportunity to earn $100 a night; or a watch to remind you to talk about the flexibility of being a consultant. Put an item in each of the remaining bags that will remind you to talk about the different benefits of your product and your business.

Think about the things that make your product unique and special. Number the bags on the outside 1-10. This is so you can put the items in the different bags in the order you want to talk about them. The heart might go in bag #1 so you can thank your hostess and recognize her right away. Then put items in the next two bags that would remind you to talk about the benefits of your product line. You could put an item in bag #4 that is a sponsoring clue and so on.

Give each guest a bag as she arrives and tell her not to look inside yet. Then you can open the party by introducing yourself and asking, "Who has bag number one? Great! Go ahead and open your bag and take out the clue inside: not the product, just the clue—a heart! That's because hostesses are the heart of my business. Without people like Cindy, I'd be out of business! Cindy has been awesome to work with. She got me her guest list right away, called all of you to tell you how great the product is and invited you to her party. Also, Cindy got five outside orders. Thank you, Cindy! But you all know Cindy better than I do. What do you love about Cindy?"

Let several people share what they love about Cindy. At this point, everyone in the room wants to be Cindy! Who doesn't love public appreciation and praise? This is your first booking seed. Then say "Now let's talk a little bit about the product in your bag." Ask, "Who has this product? How do you use it?" Let people share their ideas and move on to the next bag. "Okay, who has bag number two?" and go through the same process.

**Important tip:** Your guests are much more credible than you are when talking about your product. In your guests' eyes, they are just sharing what they love about your product. They also know you are there to sell. You can share eighteen ways to use this product or that product. However, a guest saying "Oh I love it, I use it every day!" will sell ten times more than you talking about the same product. Let them sell your product for you. It is faster, more profitable and more fun for your guests.

The gift bag party is fun, fast and easy! You walk in with ten gift bags, set them down and you are set up. There are lots of fun party ideas like this one, and the gift bag party and the next one, party cards, are my two favorites.

I used party cards the last five years that I was in the field and holding 150 to 175 parties per year. They are so easy! You have ten cards numbered 1-10 for the guests. Each guest gets a card when she arrives. You introduce yourself and ask who has card #1. The guest reads her card that says "Star of the Show" on the front. You also have ten cards that tell you how to respond to the guest cards. Your card #1 says, "Bring hostess up front and thank her in a big way!" When you bring the hostess up front and tell everyone in the room how much you appreciate her, how awesome she is and how great she has been to work with, not only do you make the hostess feel really special, you begin to create a desire in the guests to be recognized in that same manner.

Next, your card tells you to ask the guest to read the back of her card. The back of the guest's card says. "Ask hostess about her wish list."

Then you ask the hostess to share what she wants to get with her free product, half-priced items and so on. You are only on card #1 and you have already planted two booking seeds.

The next thing on your card is, "Ask guest (who had card #1) to pick a product she would like to hear about." She chooses a product from your display and you share a little bit about that product. Then you move on to card #2 in the same manner.

The cards are your presentation. When you are done with the cards, you are done with your presentation. It takes about thirty minutes, plants over twenty booking seeds and over thirty recruiting seeds! The cards are fun, fast and easy. You can even use the party cards with the gift bag party and put one of the guest cards in each bag instead of a clue. You can find the party cards on my website at www.averagetoexcellence.com.

These are just a couple of fun, interactive party ideas that make doing the presentation part of a party so easy. You don't have to remember what to say—just follow the clues or the cards. That makes it easier for you to relax, smile and have fun. When you are doing that, it's contagious and your guests will do the same.

## Stacking the Hostess

Another great way to build desire around booking parties is to stack the hostess. Pick someone in the room to be a pretend hostess. Then explain the hostess plan to the group. As you share the dollar amount of free product an average hostess receives, you will literally put that dollar amount of product in the pretend hostess's hands. Then as you share how many half-priced items they receive, put that number of half-priced items in her hands. If there is a hostess special going on, share that and put the special in her hands. It is very visual and powerful! Most people are visual learners. When you tell them that your average hostess receives $100 in free product and three half-priced items, they think "Oh that's nice." However, it doesn't really register. Showing them what they get is much more powerful than just talking about it!

**Important tip:** Start with the half-priced items and choose the most expensive things on your table. When choosing the free product, choose your least expensive items on the table. This gets more products in your pretend hostess's hands and makes hosting a party more desirable. You'll also want to choose the products. When you let the pretend hostess choose, it takes too long.

It is important to talk in dollars and not percentages when you do this. People don't relate to percentages—they often think it's just a discount. For example say, "With a $400 party you receive $80 in free product" instead of saying "twenty percent in free product."

If your company offers booking gifts when the hostess gets bookings at her party, remember to say, "Mary gets this special gift when two people book a party tonight." Remember that people book parties to help a friend!

### Be Sure to Include a Booking Game

One of the easiest and most powerful ways to leave each party with multiple bookings is to play some kind of booking game. I usually played a booking game right after "stack the hostess." You'll be surprised at the level of enthusiasm and fun a booking game brings to your parties. People like to play games, take a chance and win a prize. There are lots of booking games you can play and most work well. My favorite—and the one that took my personal calendar from 13 parties to 36 in thirty days and over 50 parties on my calendar by the second month—was the dice game. I was able to give away

20-30 parties to my team every month! Not only did it explode my calendar, as I taught it to consultants and leaders in my downline, our team sales exploded as well.

With the dice game there are eleven envelopes. Each envelope has a card in it. Some of the envelopes say, "win a prize," one says "grand prize" and some say "book a party." If a guest chooses to play, she rolls the dice and receives the envelope with the matching number. For the prizes, I used goodie bags with inexpensive gifts (each under a dollar) in them. You can use candy bars, inexpensive samples your company might sell to you at a discount or little gifts you pick up at the dollar store. The grand prize should have a twenty to thirty dollar perceived value. You can find the Dice Game Kit on my website at www.averagetoexcellence.com. It includes detailed instructions on how to play, including a CD where I role-play the game. It is so good that three companies have purchased it for their starter kits!

## The Opportunity to Earn Free Product Is a Big Motivator

This is especially true when the product a guest wants is more than her budget allows. Adding higher-priced items to the kit that you take to your parties will get some of those high-ticket items into your guests' hands. They are more likely to book a party if they fall in love with something they can't afford. Seeing the more expensive items in person is powerful. Those are the items you want to talk about at your parties!

If your company offers a hostess special, take advantage of that. Order it ahead of time and take it to your parties. Seeing the special in a flyer is one thing. Seeing it in person is quite another. Specials can increase your bookings, especially if you have them at your parties.

## Final Thoughts

There are four last tips I'd like to share with you that will help you book more parties at your parties:

**1. Plant booking seeds throughout your party.** These are subtle hints that remind them that booking a party is a good idea. Your party cards or items in the gift bags will do some of this for you, and you can still sprinkle more in!

Here are four sample booking seeds:

- "This is one of the products my hostesses choose most often for their half-priced item." That reminds guests that hostesses get half-priced items.
- "If you see something you like, remember every product has three prices: full price, half price and free!"
- "Isn't it nice to take a break and have some girlfriend time?"
- "This is on Mary's wish list to get as one of her free products."

**2. Walk your customers through the customer information card if your company provides one.** If you ask customers to fill it out, you'll get very few back, and the ones you do get will probably be incomplete. If you don't have a customer information card at your company, I encourage you to create your own. See the template at the end of this chapter. Walking them through the questions gives you one more chance to sell the hostess opportunity. You can say something like this when you get to the "host a party" question: "Remember how much product Anna had in her arms when we did the pretend hostess? If you'd like to host a party and get all of that product, put a checkmark on #3."

**3. Ask for the booking when they are checking out.** Ask each guest about a booking even if she checked no on her customer information card. Guests may be thinking about having a party and they don't want to tell you because they haven't decided quite yet. You can say,

"I see you checked 'no' on the information card regarding having a party. Does that mean 'no not ever' or 'no not now?'" You'll be surprised how many people say "Oh no, I just can't do it this month, but I'd be interested in doing a party next month!"

When you look at your customer information cards as part of the checkout process, you'll be surprised to find that many people don't buy their favorite item. Maybe they could only afford one thing and they needed a gift, so they purchased something for someone else. Perhaps the item they loved was out of their budget. When you see they didn't get their favorite item, you can say, "I see that the _____ is your favorite product. Would you like to get that for free?" Most of the time, asking someone directly is what it takes to get the booking. If you're waiting for them to tell you that they want to host a party, you'll have a pretty empty calendar!

**4. Do an excellent job of hostess coaching.** That's the key to high attendance. No matter how well you do these other steps, if you only have three people at a party, it will be difficult to get three bookings. If you have ten guests at your party and follow these steps you'll easily leave with three or more bookings.

To positively impact bookings at your parties, do fun, interactive events, play booking games, bring higher-priced items and hostess specials to the parties, plant booking seeds, ask everyone for bookings and do an excellent job of hostess coaching! By including as many of these tools in each and every party you do, you will be booking lots of parties at your parties.

## Customer Information Card

Front · Back

Customer Information Card

Name:_____ Date:_____

Address:_____

City/State:_____ Zip:_____

Phone: Day_____ Evening_____

Email:_____

Hostess:_____

My favorite item was_____

☐ Please notify me of product specials and other offers.

☐ I would like to receive a gift for each person I refer who becomes a hostess or consultant.

☐ I would like to host a party.

☐ I would like more information about earning income, prizes, awards and trips to exotic locations.

☐ I would book a party if the hostess decides to become a consultant.

Hostess referrals:

| | Name | Phone Number: |
|---|---|---|
| 1. | | |
| 2. | | |
| 3. | | |
| 4. | | |
| 5. | | |
| 6. | | |

Consultant referrals:

| | Name | Phone Number: |
|---|---|---|
| 1. | | |
| 2. | | |
| 3. | | |
| 4. | | |
| 5. | | |
| 6. | | |

## Ask For The Booking

ASK for the booking! ASK EACH GUEST. Even if they checked "no" on their customer information card, they may be thinking about having a party, they just don't want to tell you, because they haven't decided yet.

You can say, "I see you checked 'no' on the information card to having a party…does that mean no not ever, or no not now." You'll be surprised how many people say, "Oh no, I just can't do it this month…but I'd be interested in doing a party next month!"

You'll also be surprised at how many people don't buy their favorite item when you look at their customer information card. Maybe they could only afford one thing and they needed a gift, so they purchased something for someone else, or the item they loved was out of their budget.

When you see that they didn't get their favorite item, you can say, "I see that the (whatever the item is), is your favorite product. Would you like to get that for free?" Most of the time asking someone directly is what it takes to get the booking.

# 19: PRIORITIZING: THE KEY TO SANITY AND MAXIMUM RESULTS

Most of us are overwhelmed by all the things we need to accomplish and are responsible for today, this week and this month. However, we all have 24 hours in a day, and there are things we can do that will put us back in control of our time.

## Living Beyond "Reactive Mode"

One of our biggest time stealers is living in reactive mode. When we are doing this, we answer every call, say yes to any and every request, and so on. Stephen Covey, author of *7 Habits of Highly Effective People*, used the following exercise to illustrate this point.

Covey placed a wide-mouth gallon jar on a table. Next to the jar sat a collection of fist-sized rocks. He carefully filled the jar with the big rocks until no more would fit. Looking up, he asked the group, "Is the jar full?"

Everyone responded, "Yes."

Next, he pulled a large bowl of gravel from under the table and proceeded to gently pour the gravel into the jar. The gravel settled into the spaces between the rocks. Again he queried, "Is the jar full?"

"Probably not," was the group's more hesitant reply.

Reaching under the table again, he withdrew a bowl filled with sand. Slowly, he dumped the sand into the jar. The sand filled the spaces not occupied by the rocks and the gravel. Once more, he asked, "Is the jar full?"

Catching on to the demonstration, the audience agreed, "No."

Finally, Covey reached for a pitcher of water and poured water into the jar until it was filled to the top. Looking up at the group, the time management guru asked, "What is the point of my illustration?"

One man replied, "No matter how full your schedule is, you can always fit one more thing into it."

"No!" the guru responded. *"The point of this illustration is: If you don't put the big rocks in first, you'll never get them in at all!"* Covey wanted his audience to understand this tip: Get the important things figured out first, then fit everything else in around them. In other words, know what your priorities are.

What are your big rocks: children, spouse, church, business? What else? It is important to prioritize your big rocks. So, how do you get started?

### Start with your planner

The first tool that you will need for prioritizing your "rocks" is a functional planner. You can purchase a planner or work with one that is accessible on a hand-held device. Use the method that you feel works best for you. Ideally, your planner includes month-at-a-glance pages, weekly schedule pages, and daily schedule pages. Take the time to organize each section.

On the month-at-a-glance page, mark days for general activities, regularly scheduled events, or unique occasions. Use different colored highlighters to identify different categories of activities. Use the highlighters to box the various days. You could use a red highlighter (for the heart) to mark family time as important days on which you don't want to book a party. Don't necessarily note Johnny's soccer practice. Do note events such as your daughter's birthday or your date night with hubby. Use a blue highlighter (for business) to mark your meeting days. Use a green highlighter (for money) to mark your party days; include those days already scheduled as well as the days you want to fill.

Use the weekly section of your planner to list your priorities for that week. This is the location to include details such as "clean kitchen cupboards" or "have lunch with mom."

On the daily section, list specific priorities for that day. Use the hourly schedule to plan time to tackle individual priorities listed for the day.

When we go through one day without a plan, we miss opportunities to do important things. The day just goes right by us. Let me share an example of how I planned my day to include three of my top priorities. For years I had coffee with my husband between 6:30 and 7:30 in the morning. From 3:30-4:30 in the afternoon, I played Sequence® over tea with my youngest daughter, Carli. After my time with Carli, I would get ready to go to my party. I also scheduled my phone calls between 6:00 and 8:00 p.m. on weeknights when I didn't have a party. As Carli grew and had her own work schedule, I rescheduled my teatime with her according to her work hours. I planned my hourly schedule around these three priorities every day. By deliberately scheduling these priorities, I made sure the important things got done first. Then if I ran out of time, I had only the least important things left undone.

Sometimes, I get too busy being reactive to make my lists and plan my day. When I begin to feel overwhelmed, my husband always asks, "Have you made your list yet?" Of course, when I do take the time to make the list and schedule my day, I feel so much better. It may be a hectic day, but if I have a plan, I feel back in control.

Sit down and consider what your priorities are. If you have a job, schedule your priorities against the job schedule. If you are scheduling around children, pay for childcare a couple of hours a day or at least a few times a week. If paying for childcare is not an option for you, plan with your spouse to work in your business time, or perhaps trade childcare with another mom in order to free up business time for your week.

Even with detailed planning, so many things can come up in a day to get us off track from our plan. Some things are out of our control, but some time stealers can be taken back under our own control.

## Time Stealers

Time stealers are those tasks that are often necessary tasks, yet need to be managed. If these tasks are not managed, they make us inefficient and they steal valuable time. Here are a few of the time stealers you will want to manage well.

- **Phone:** It is easy to step into the trap of picking up every call when it comes in. Before we know it, an unexpected call will eat up valuable time that had been set aside for some other priority. Make a habit of screening all your phone calls. Then return those calls during your scheduled office hours. Prioritizing the calls according to your priority list will allow you to return calls according to the greatest need. With that plan, you will be able to take control of the phone.
- **Television:** The average person watches three hours of TV per day. Is there something more productive you can do with that time? If

there is something you specifically want to see, certainly watch it! However, scrolling through the channels looking for something to watch is a time stealer.

- **Email:** Email is certainly a great way to communicate, especially when you need to communicate with many people at once. It is also a useful alternative when you don't have time for a longer phone conversation. It's the ongoing emailing conversations back and forth with friends and family that eats away at your time. One of the time management books I read suggested checking email once in the morning and once mid-afternoon. My last CEO followed this pattern consistently. We knew he would be checking email within a few hours and we didn't expect an instant reply. If it were urgent, we knew we could reach him on his cell. You may think that people will feel you are not available if you limit email time. However, if you establish this habit and are consistent, people will learn not to expect an immediate response.

- **Technology tools:** As technology advances, we have to learn to use those tools efficiently so that they do not become time stealers.
  - > Texting: This can be a quick and easy way to communicate unless it becomes a back and forth thirty-minute dialogue. Treat texting as you would a phone call. You have the luxury of "screening" for immediate need. If it can wait, then return these messages just as you do your phone calls. If it is an urgent situation, handle it immediately or text the person to let them know how soon you can get back to them.
  - > Social media like Facebook®, Twitter®, and LinkedIn®: They can be a good source of exposure. Again, check in twice a day. In the morning, add a positive quote or thought that will make you stand out. In the evening, update with an occasional bit about your business. Don't get caught up in spending hours and hours on social media. See the chapters about how to work with Facebook effectively in Part Three of this book.

> Surfing the Web: Again, there are great resources and tools on the Internet. However, don't let purposeless surfing eat up valuable time in your day.

## Time Builders

In contrast to time stealer habits, some habits actually deliver time-building benefits. By practicing these habits, you will find that you can accomplish more in less time.

- **Read.** Take time to self-train. It is a valuable use of your time. Be a lifelong learner. The more you learn, the more you earn. There are so many great books and CDs that can really make a difference in the way we think, work, train and LIVE! Schedule time every day to read or listen. Just fifteen minutes can make a difference.
- **Listen.** Turn your car into a traveling university. Listen to a training CD in your car instead of music.
- **Coordinate.** Group similar activities together. Instead of pulling everything out to make enough hostess packets or recruiting packets for tonight's party, schedule a period of time to make packets. If you're going to gather everything to make packets, make twenty or thirty to cover the need for several parties. Grouping activities is more efficient and eliminates the stress of trying to get everything done right before a party. Better yet, hire a school child to do this for you.
- **Schedule.** In your planner, schedule weekly time to make booking and hostess coaching contacts. Schedule one hour a day to work your business in order to grow your business quickly. Then, stick to your scheduled plan.
- **Prepare.** When making copies of frequently used handouts—such as flyers for monthly specials, packets or guest folders—make a minimum of 25 copies of each. This habit will save you from frequent trips to the copy center.

- **Utilize.** Adjust to unexpected situations, tap resources and make the most of extra minutes.

  > When you have a cancellation, utilize the time you would have been gone to work your business. Use the time to make booking, sponsoring and hostess coaching contacts or to make packets and guest folders. This time was scheduled to work, so use it for that purpose.

  > Children love to help! Utilize their enthusiasm. When my kids were little, they loved to label catalogs, brochures and postcards for me. As they got older, they put packets together for me. Eventually, of course, I had to pay them, but it was still more efficient for me to pay them a small fee to do those things and spend my time on more revenue-generating activity such as booking and hostess coaching calls.

  > Utilize a few extra minutes to gain some uninterrupted time. I used to leave thirty minutes early for my parties so I could stop somewhere like a coffee shop or parking lot and make thirty minutes of uninterrupted calls. I was leaving the house that night anyway, and I found that thirty minutes of uninterrupted time very useful.

- **Finalize.** Complete a task before moving to the next task. For instance, if a customer care call turns into an order, complete the call, write up the order, place the order, file the order and send an email or card letting the customer know it's been ordered and when she can expect delivery. Then move on to the next task.

- **Delegate.** Working with priorities will increase your income more quickly. Increased income can buy you more time. If you earned $1,000 per month, could you hire someone to clean your house or mow your grass? As your income grows, could you hire an assistant to make hostess packets, enter orders, and so on? If your income grew to $2,000 or $5,000, look at paying someone else to do things that would free up your time. My friend, Leigh, who earned over $1 million a year in direct sales, told me many years ago when her income was much less, *"If more money won't buy me more time, I don't need more money!"*

- **Consider.** What is your prime time? We are more productive in our prime time. Are you a morning person or an evening person? What is your best working time? I tried to schedule my calls after 10:00 a.m., because I knew early morning was not my prime time. Be sure you are working when it is your best time to work!

## Getting Organized

Now, let's talk about some things you can do that will help you to be more organized. These tips will save you time, help you to feel more structured and give you more control of your business. Whether your home office is a separate room or a kitchen table, getting organized is the key.

- Keep your workspace neat and tidy. Clutter can make you feel overwhelmed and you can waste time looking through piles of paper over and over for different documents and notes.
- Invest in a file cabinet or file box for easy access.
- Find a storage place for everything and keep it close where you will be more likely to use it.
- Keep everything you need to make hostess packets, recruiting packets, and guest folders in accordion files or file boxes. When it's time to make packets, everything is in one place.
- Keep receipts in a small accordion file. Label each section for easy reference, such as hostess gifts, postage, product for my kit, copies, travel and meals, office supplies. Create a spreadsheet to track your expenses. At the end of the year, total the columns to see your expenses for tax purposes.
- Keep a small spiral notebook or an inexpensive mileage log in your car to track your mileage. Your mileage is a tax deduction. Record driving mileage for parties, meetings, trips to pick up office supplies or to make copies, and other business-related trips.

- Simplify your party to make your life easier.
  - > Take ten to fifteen sample items. Tell your guests if there is something you don't have with you tonight, you can bring it to their party when they book.
  - > Ask the hostess how many guests she is expecting so you can come prepared with enough guest folders.
  - > Take six hostess packets and three recruiting packets into each party and keep more in the car. This will save you the time and money of mailing them if you don't have enough.
  - > Keep everything for your kit together in one place. It can be stressful looking for a particular product as you're trying to get out the door to your party. As your budget allows, purchase doubles of the things you want for personal use, so you can keep your kit product together and available.
  - > Have a checklist of things you need for each party that you can double check before you leave the house. Include things like:
    - Display accessories
    - Pens
    - Guest folders
    - Hostess and recruiting packets
    - Calculator
    - Money bag with change
    - Product
    - Raffle tickets
    - Prizes
    - Anything you need for every party

## Time Management Success

We all want to be successful. We all want to make a difference. We all want to feel balanced. We just have to plan for it. Plan your work and work your plan! Take the time to really consider personal and business priorities and plan them into the day, week or month.

Then you will get that feeling of balance and success. After taking advantage of time builders and managing time stealers, you will appreciate the positive accomplishments you make each day. Now that you are ready to think about your priorities, consider these helpful acronyms as you plan in your business goals:

- ROTI: Return on time invested
- DIMM: Does it make me money
- DIBB: Does it build my business

Time management and prioritizing will make your life less stressful and more productive. Success happens when you focus the full power of all you are on what you have a burning desire to achieve!

| Sample Month at-a-glance | | | October | | | |
|---|---|---|---|---|---|---|
| **Sun** | **Mon** | **Tue** | **Wed** | **Thu** | **Fri** | **Sat** |
| | | | 1 | | 2 Date w/hubby | 3 11a-Barbara 3p-Susie 7p-Nikki |
| 4 Family day | 5 6:30p-Liz | 6 6:30p (Still need to book) | 7 | 8 | 9 Date w/hubby | 10 |
| 11 Family day | 12 7p-Unit Meeting | 13 | 14 | 15 | 16 Date w/hubby | 17 11a-Jenny 3p-Alexa 7p-Melissa |
| 18 Family day | 19 | 20 | 21 | 22 | 23 Date w/hubby | 24 |
| 25 Family day | 26 6:30p-Jill | 27 6:30p-Mandy | 28 | 29 | 30 Date w/hubby | 31 |

# Sample Daily Planner

## Tuesday, October 13

| To Do List | Appointments |
|---|---|
| Close Mary's party | 8a |
| Follow-up with Jill | 9a |
| Pick up dry cleaning | 10a |
| Grocery shop | 11a |
| Mail hostess packet to Lori | 12p |
|  | 1p |
|  | 2p   Parent-teacher conference |
|  | 3p |
|  | 4p   Pickup Carli from swim practice |
|  | 5p |
|  | 6p |
|  | 7p   Booking calls |
|  | 8p |
|  | 9p |
|  | 10p |

# PART THREE:
## Build Your Business
## Using FACEBOOK®

# 20: USING FACEBOOK® TO GET BETTER BOOKING AND SPONSORING RESULTS

Booking parties today is a big area of concern, given that it has become harder than ever to get bookings, not just for new people but for very seasoned consultants and leaders as well. In fact, top sellers—people who never had any difficulty booking parties—are finding it challenging. Even when you do get bookings, they often cancel.

In a previous chapter, "Getting More Bookings in Today's Market" on page 59, I covered understanding today's market and how to use the phone more effectively, as well as how to incorporate email and texting to get the results you want. Facebook is another important tool that can be very effective in today's market.

I do have to tell you that I am one of those people who used to be very resistant to Facebook. For the last several years, I was training people to avoid Facebook. I saw it as a time stealer. People get on there and they spend their entire day on Facebook.

However, what I have learned from some very, very successful people in the business is that it is a great platform to market your business, to get bookings and for sponsoring. It's working. In fact it's not just working, it's working very well. I can't believe I am actually saying this: *It is a better way to book parties today than the telephone.* The market may shift again and the telephone may come back and be a better way to book parties. It's just not the case right now.

I've been in direct sales since 1985 and I've always trained on that personal touch, the importance of booking calls, as well as personal invitations and reminder calls from the hostess. What I have learned from my coaching clients, team mentor groups and from interviewing a number of people in direct selling—as well as people outside of direct sales—is that for most people, there isn't enough time for all of that today.

I am seeing direct sellers who are using Facebook effectively fill their calendars quickly. They are booking four, five and six parties in a week rather than one or two. Their calendars are exploding. What is even better is that they are sponsoring not only one new consultant a week, many of them are sponsoring two, three, four, five or even six new consultants in a week using texting and Facebook.

My daughter Carli recently signed up to be a direct sales consultant and you might think, "Of course, Carli is going to have success because her mom is a direct selling trainer." However, even though Carli grew up with direct sales, she has not really had the opportunity to hear me train people. She's our customer service person. Another staff person edits our calls and so he hears all of my trainings and could probably recite them word for word. However, Carli hasn't had that opportunity. Given that, she was starting out fresh, just like you might be doing.

Let me share her initial results with you. She got seven bookings in one weekend. She got zero bookings on the phone, two bookings through email, four bookings on Facebook and one through text messaging. All I did was coach her on the phone Saturday afternoon because she had gotten discouraged Friday night and had called me because she wasn't getting any bookings from her many phone calls. We spent about ten minutes talking about how to use Facebook, texting and email. That night, she got seven bookings using those three tools. Those are excellent results, and you can do that too!

## Use Facebook Chat to Book Parties

Facebook is a great tool to use to widen your circle of contacts and get yourself known as someone that people like and trust. Below are ten tips on how to do that. However, before we go there, here is how you can use one particular Facebook tool to actually get parties on your calendar directly.

Chat is a very effective way to book parties because you have a captive audience sitting there looking for social interactions. They are usually appreciative to see the chat window pop up. You can use Facebook chat just like you would use the telephone. When you see someone is on Facebook, start chatting with them and use the "take a break from the madness, escape the chaos, getting together for a fun evening with their girlfriends" approach, just as you would if you were on the phone with them. See the chapter on "Getting More Bookings in Today's Market" on page 59.

I became a really huge fan of this particular part of Facebook chat when I was on an extensive road trip. The only time I was on my laptop was late in the evening, which is when I would check my emails and spend some time on Facebook. One night at about 10:00 p.m., a home office executive connected with me and said, "We've been to your website. We're very interested in talking to you about speaking at our conference." I was impressed, to say the least. I realized if that is going to happen to me, then direct sellers can certainly use this tool to book parties.

When you're on Facebook, you can see all of your friends that are online. Find someone in the chat list that is online and with whom you have a connection, and start a chat conversation. It could be about booking a party, about an existing party that you know they are possibly attending, or you could even talk about your business opportunity. The great thing is that they know that you can see that they're there on Facebook. They almost have to respond, whereas with email or even with calling on the phone or texting, you don't know if they are checking their email or texts or available to talk. Facebook chat can be a great place to connect and to book those parties. Just use the appropriate approach and script, just as you would on the phone, or even in person.

## How to Use Facebook Effectively

The main thing to understand about using Facebook to get bookings is that this is a communications medium. It enables people to get to know, like and trust you. Once they do, they will be curious about your business and will reach out to *you*. Here are a dozen tips on using Facebook to grow your business.

**1. Be yourself.** The secret to standing out among the tens of millions of people on Facebook is to simply be yourself. Express your thoughts your way. Share things that you believe will be of interest to your audience. Allow your unique voice and brand to emerge, with the goal of having your friends comment on your postings.

**2. Brand yourself.** You will do this through your posts, comments and pictures. For example, one of my Facebook friends is a Christian direct sales speaker. Her posts are often a short passage of scripture or a positive quote. Whatever she posts is always uplifting so you want to read her posts. That is her brand. One of my Facebook mentors, Barbie Collins Young, is a comic, a marathon runner and a dedicated mommy. That is her brand, so many of her posts are comical. Her profile pictures reflect her brand as well, with pictures of her and her son Findley in a race or doing something funny. In fact, I can remember one profile picture of Barbie leaping over a fire in her marathon gear, complete with number and all muddy from the race. Funny and athletic.

My oldest daughter Jillian is all about fun, family and girlfriends! Her profile pictures are of her and her girlfriends having a great time, or Jillian and her niece Isabelle, or with her husband Mike doing something silly and fun. Both Barbie and Jillian are two examples of people who do a fabulous job of branding themselves.

**3. Encourage comments.** You'll know if your postings are effective or interesting if people comment on them. If nobody comments, you might want to ask some friends who've had good results on getting responses to their posts for help or get more friends on Facebook. By having a larger number of Facebook friends, you are more likely to have people comment. For instance, as I mentioned, Barbie—who has been a great mentor to me on using Facebook—is a comic. One of the things that Barbie is most loved for is her fantastic sense of humor. One of her posts was a video of her home. She was just walking around her home, which is basically a luxurious estate, being very fun and lighthearted. She would say things like, "This is my wine cellar and this is my kitchen and this is my office." This could have come across as a little ostentatious or even as somewhat arrogant except that, at the very end and in typical Barbie style, she said, "This is my indoor hot tub, and this is my . . .whoops!" and she just falls into the pool while she's videotaping! It was hysterical. I don't even remember how many comments she got to that post but it was one of the most highly commented posts I've ever seen. Basically, she was advertising the fantastic home that her business paid for. However, she turned that into a funny thing by falling into the pool. One of her posts the other day was: "Tried yoga today, found stress to be more fun." That's Barbie's brand. She's a comic.

Personally, I like to make people laugh. I am by no means a comic like my friend Barbie. I don't have a witty bone in my body. However, let's just be honest, I do so many funny things that I can write about and I make people chuckle. As a result, I get lots of comments on my posts. For example, I was already on my way to the chiropractor when I realized I had on one brown shoe and one black shoe. I also posted the true story about standing in front of my door with a bag of groceries in my arms, trying to open my door with my car remote. It took me about five seconds before I realized a key works better than the remote. My friends had a field day with those posts on Facebook!

I have other friends on Facebook that very often share quotes that make you stop and think, or sometimes they post funny passages. I always read those posts. Some people post videos all the time, whether the videos are their own or something they found interesting on the Internet and wanted to share on Facebook.

**4. Balance business with personal posts.** Whenever you type into that area on your profile page that says, "What's on your mind?", you are making a post on Facebook. This is what people will see in their News Feed. I recommend a minimum ratio of one to ten (one business posting to ten personal ones). Just posting business announcements and offers (or even half business and half personal) can look like spam, and people will hide your posts or even "unfriend" you if all you are talking about on Facebook is business. However, interspersing some subtle business references amongst your personal postings and comments will help people see you as a real person, and that builds trust. Your business postings can be subtle, like this one from my friend Lindsey Hale, "So ladies, I know you got paid today. What did you do with your check?" She had received 36 comments when I saw it, ranging from "I treated myself to a manicure/pedicure", "I paid off my minivan", to "I paid for my nephews mission trip". It's a business post, *and* it catches your attention. In fact, she recruited two people that day as a result of her post.

Make sure you do not use any part of your business name in the name you use on your personal profile. Facebook will shut you down.

**5. Use pictures to get noticed.** This is the eye candy, and helps your posts get noticed. You can also change your profile picture regularly and people will notice and comment. Barbie's a great example here. She changes her profile picture frequently using some great fun photos.

**6. Consistently build your Friends list.** Set a goal for a number of friends to add per day, maybe five or ten. Let's talk about the Friend Finder tool on Facebook. That's a great resource to use to update your contact list. You can put in places that you worked, schools you attended, jobs that you've had and so on. It will collect people for you and when you recognize a name, send a friend request to them. If you aren't sure they'll remember you, make sure you send a message as well, reminding them who you are and how you know each other.

At your parties, ask each guest if they use Facebook and *then* send them friend requests when you get home. Also, you can look on your Facebook friends' lists for people you might already know but have not added yet. Be careful about sending friend requests to people who do not know you at all. Some people are wary of adding people as a Facebook friend that they don't know. Bottom line: the more friends you have, the better. You are building your prospect database!

**7. Make comments.** Here is where your Facebook presence comes alive. Leave comments that spur other people on to make their own comments. That's how they get to know, like and trust you. Also, make sure that you go back and comment on the comments people make on your posts. Try to be the last person to comment.

You can quickly go back to the posts you commented on—they are all posted in your Notifications. You will be notified when someone comments on the same thing you did. Just click on the notification and like Dorothy in Kansas, whoosh—you are right back to their site.

**8. Be careful what you post on other people's walls.** When you write on somebody's wall, it's public to her friends and yours! Make sure that what you post on someone else's profile/wall is appropriate for both audiences. That's one mistake that I see people make. When it happens, I just cringe and think, "Oh, I know you didn't mean for everybody to see that." Here's an example of an appropriate and effective wall post that was put on a friend's wall. Lynn noticed on her friend's wall that people were talking about needing extra money. She commented that they could check out her company and she shared her personal website. Guess what? That person signed up! Lynn sponsored somebody in another state that she'd never even met.

**9. Be indirect in your references to your business on your personal profile page.** For example, you could say something like, "I'm so excited because I booked our Disney vacation today and it only cost me $300, thanks to XYZ Company." Or, "I love my job." Or, how about this? "Woohoo! I earned a free trip to Mexico. Thank you XYZ Company." That's a good recruiting post. It is subtle and just might get someone's attention. Perhaps you could make a lifestyle post like, "Nothing like my Tuesdays. I get a pedicure while someone else cleans my house." You don't even have to mention your company. People may start to wonder how you can afford a housekeeper. Perhaps you have a personal trainer. You can mention that in a post. When my friend, Lindsey, paid off her student loan thanks to her business, she posted that. That created lots of questions because many of her college friends still had a long time left on their own loans.

**10. Post regularly and consistently.** Set aside twenty minutes in the morning and twenty minutes in the evening. You can even set a timer and when the alarm goes off, you move on to other things on your to do list. Make a post on your wall and reply to comments made to your previous posts.

**11. Use your personal page** to market your business in the ways I have shared above. If you have a professional page and only use it to market your business, the only people who see those posts are the people who know they are interested in your product and company and have "liked" your page. You lose the opportunity to market to the masses and generate interest with new people. Although on Facebook you have the option to create a professional page, if you limit your business posts to 10% of your overall posts, using your personal page to market your business is a more effective strategy.

**12. Have fun.** Facebook is a great tool to use on many levels. It can be a lot of fun connecting with people, expanding your circle of friends and learning new things. People will notice that you are having fun and they will want to connect with you. That is what you want, and that is what can help you build your business.

# 21: COACHING YOUR HOSTESS USING FACEBOOK®

The key to being successful is making things fun, fast and easy. Think of Facebook as the new email. In fact, it is a combination of email, texting and Evites®—all in one place. Originally, many people thought that Facebook was just for young people. However, moms and grandmas are using Facebook to communicate with their kids and grandkids. Many businesses have business pages and advertise on Facebook. Older people are having fun reconnecting with old friends and relatives that they haven't seen or talked to in years. Many of us had to learn to text to talk to our teenagers. Now we're learning that we have to use Facebook to communicate with them.

I would encourage you to open up Facebook on your computer so that, as I explain things, you can be online and see exactly what I am talking about.

## Why Is Facebook a Good Place to Hostess Coach?

I have interviewed a lot of consultants and leaders on this topic, and I have bought a lot of materials on how to effectively use social media. One of the people I interviewed has had an amazing amount of success using Facebook for her hostess coaching. Her name is Tanya Branch and she shared with me some statistics that you might find useful.

In September, 2010, Tanya sold $7,496 and held 16 parties with 117 guests. In October, she sold $10,331 with 19 parties and 142 guests. She produced these results through hostess coaching on Facebook. In November, she sold $13,103 with 24 parties and 177 guests. In December, where we can only sell for two weeks before the deadline for holiday delivery, she sold $5,811 and held 12 parties with 79 guests. That's $36,741 in sales in the last four months of the year with 71 parties and 515 guests, with an average guest attendance of 7.25. When I was with this company, my average party sales total was $350. This is not a company with a giant party average. This is someone who is getting great results working in a new innovative way, with average sales per year for the last four years of $70,000.

Tanya isn't the only one having tremendous success. Hostess coaching using Facebook is in fact, another piece of the market shift that is happening in our business. With 23 to 30-year-old hostesses, Facebook is the way they communicate and invite people to events. Even with older hostesses, it can be an additional way for them to invite more guests and have bigger and more successful parties.

Everyone knows what Facebook is, and most people use it in some capacity. It is not a foreign word to anybody. With Facebook, everyone's reconnecting. What better way to get some of your old high school friends together than by having a party and inviting them on Facebook?

It is important to note that most people who have Facebook Accounts also have smart phones, and Facebook is an application on their phone. This makes it easy to reach everyone in one quick step. A hostess doesn't have to figure out whether to text her friends, call them or use Facebook, because she can do all of that with one simple step on Facebook. Hostess coaching on Facebook is fun, fast and easy, and it doesn't make having a party appear time-consuming for your hostess.

## First Steps

**Get connected.** When you book a party, some of the first questions to ask the hostess is, "Are you on Facebook? How do you want to invite your guests?" Give them options. You can say, "Would you like to use Evites, a Facebook event, email or mail invitations, or a little bit of everything?" This gets easier once you've done this for a while because the person you're talking to was probably invited via a Facebook event invitation. However, if you don't offer it, or if your hostess is not that comfortable with Facebook, she may not even think of that as an option.

Make sure you have your hostess's email address and phone number in case you can't find them on Facebook. You might want to ask, "How are you registered on Facebook?" Some people use their maiden names as their middle names, so make sure to ask them how they're registered.

To make this work, you and your hostess need to become "friends" on Facebook, if you aren't already. You can have her send you a friend request, or you can send her one. Once she accepts the request, or you accept hers, you can create a Facebook event for her.

**Create the event.** This is like creating an Evite or mailing out invitations. However, it only takes about five minutes. See the next chapter, "Setting Up an Event on Facebook" for detailed instructions and tips on doing this. When you are finished, just send a message to your hostess or make a post on her wall saying something like "Your event is done and you can now invite your guests."

The wall is a public communication tool. Everyone they are friends with can see what is written there. Each person has the ability to set privacy settings on their account to determine what can be seen.

People set their privacy settings when they open their accounts. When you're communicating with your hostess on a wall, it's public communication for all to see.

Once you create the event, then you implement the same three hostess coaching rules that you've always used, but without using phone calls.

**First contact.** Check back a few days after creating the Facebook event. Make sure your hostess invited her friends. You don't have to call her because you can just look at the event and see who she invited. This is just like her giving you the guest list, only now it's now on your computer screen, and nobody mailed you anything! As people start opening the event and marking their RSVPs, you'll be able to see who is coming, and if she has a lot of people under "awaiting reply." This usually means they don't often check their Facebook accounts, or they access it from their phones and don't take all of the steps necessary to access an event from a phone.

What you can do next is send a message to the folks who have not replied yet. This is like sending an email to a lot of people. It only takes about two minutes. It's fun, fast and easy, and it gets you in contact with the guests right from the start.

Go to the top of the screen and click "Message Guest." A little box will open, and it will ask you, "Do you want to message all of them, the ones that said maybe they're going to come or the not yet replied?" You can select which group of people you want to message and then type a message to the "not yet replied" group which says things similar to those you put in the information box about the event. The guests will get the message on their phone immediately. Remember, they cannot see the event through this email, so they won't know what the message means without all the information.

**Second contact.** This is when you send messages a few days before the party to remind everyone to come. We used to call and tell our hostesses to make reminder calls. Now it takes two seconds for you to do this inside the event you set up. Just follow the instructions above to create and send the reminder.

**Third contact.** This happens the day of the party. Make sure you post something on the event wall to remind everyone again. Also, make sure you post something on your wall. This is your public page, so everyone can see it. It is great advertising for your party that day. Now you'll use what is called "tagging."

Tagging is what you do when you are writing on your wall and you want it to appear on someone elses wall as well. For example, you might write "I'm so excited about Mary Cook's party tonight." If you are Facebook friends with Mary Jones, when you begin to type her name, her name will pop up. Click on her name and it will fill in on the post you are writing. Then you can finish with "I can't wait for her to go on her shopping spree!" When you publish the post, it will show up on her wall as well.

Anyone who looks at her Facebook page that day will get an automatic reminder. It is also great advertisement for your business that you are doing a party that day.

After the party, you can also send "thank you" and "thank you for attending" messages, asking those who did not attend if they want to place outside orders, and communicating with everyone your hostess invited.

It's so easy to coach your hostess all the way through using Facebook. Basically, you are talking to her friends all along the way, and you have a clear picture of how her guests are responding, their comments and questions. With which of your next hostesses are you going to use Facebook for party invites and hostess coaching?

# 22: SETTING UP AN EVENT ON FACEBOOK®

Here are the six basic steps to creating a Facebook event so that you can hostess coach and have all the communication discussed in the previous chapter. The more you play around with it, the more things you'll find that you can do.

**1. Friend request.** You can't communicate without being a friend with your hostess, so you either have to accept her friend request or send her one. That is why it is important to find out the exact name under which she is registered.

**2. Creating the event.** When you are at your computer and on Facebook, look for a link on your main page that says "Upcoming Events" on the right-hand side. Click on "See All" and then at the top, click on "Create an Event." Next, a big box opens up with a number of questions you will answer.

The first question is the date. Put in the date and the time. Then it asks, "What are you planning?" This is like the subject line of your email. Put in your hostess's name first. This is what her friends will see when they get the request. "Mary is having a party." When the guests see that, it will be exciting for them and they will open the invitation.

The next box asks for the street address. Ask your hostess if she wants the address put on the event. Don't put her street address on the invitation without her permission. The next box says "more information." This is where you type whatever you want to say about the party. Get creative. "I can't wait to show all of you the fantastic new holiday product line." Or maybe you're having a theme party. You want to make it sound fun and entertaining so they won't want to miss it. Remember to keep it short. Facebook people are into doing things fast. If it takes too long, you will lose them.

At the end, put something like, "if you cannot attend . . ." If they're attending, they won't read any further, so make sure you've covered whatever you need to cover before that. For guests who cannot attend, put ordering instructions, a link to your website, indicate that direct shipping is available, and anything else your company offers. That is your completed invitation to this event.

Next, click on "Select Guests", and a box will open with all of your contacts on Facebook. Find your hostess and select her. She is the only person you invite.

Then Facebook asks you questions at the bottom. There are four very important questions. The first question is, "Anyone can view and RSVP." The box will automatically already be checked. You want to uncheck this box, making it a private event.

The next box says "public event." Uncheck this box, again making it visible to only those invited. However, if this is a public event, like a training, an opportunity meeting or a kickoff of some kind, leave that box checked, because you want everybody to see it so they can come to your public event.

Next there is a box that asks, "Can guests invite friends?" Check this box. "Yes." You want people whom she is inviting to invite others. We always encourage friends to bring a friend. Facebook makes that easy for you.

Then there is a box for "show the guest list on the event page." Check that box. You want everyone who's coming to see who else is coming so they won't want to miss out. What this means is that everyone your hostess invites will appear on the screen.

After that, you can add a photo. Click on "Event Photo." Have some pictures on your computer of your products or whatever you would like them to see. When you click on this box, the computer will allow you to browse and find pictures that are already on your computer. Select the one you want and it will automatically be loaded into your event.

Lastly, click on "Create Event" at the bottom, and Facebook creates the event for you. All of the information you have typed in becomes your invitation.

Now click on "Select Guests." A box will come up with your name and that of your hostess. Make your hostess an "Admin" by clicking on the "Make Admin" button that appears next to her name. This will then change the event to say "created by you and your hostess." Now she can invite all of her friends, and the invitation will come from her, not from you.

**3. Posting on your wall.** You are now done with the actual event setup, and there is one more important thing to do. Click on the name of your hostess, and you will find yourself on her wall. Remember that this is for all to see. You're making a public post, and you're going to write something like "Mary, I'm so excited about your party on March 30th. I've just created your event so you can go in and invite your friends." The event is complete. Now, you continue to work with your hostess to create a successful party.

### It Really Is that Simple!

Follow the above steps and you will see how easy this is. To learn more about using Facebook, see "Facebook Do's and Don'ts" that starts on page 179, and go back and read "Coaching Your Hostess Using Facebook" for what to do after you set up the event. Meanwhile, here are some useful answers to some frequently asked questions.

**1. Why not have the hostess set up her own event?** This can work if the hostess allows guests to post photos and comments. However, in order to post messages to all guests, to get notifications when anyone posts a question or comment and to know what is going on, you need to be an administrator. If your hostess does set up the event before you do, ask her to set you up as an administrator so you can help manage the communications about the event with her guests.

**2. What do you think about using other invitation systems, including programs provided by the direct selling companies?** What I have found is that Facebook is better than invite systems that use email because many of those messages are blocked by the recipient's email service provider, don't get through at all or wind up in spam or junk mail folders. Facebook messages always get through and the recipient knows it is from someone she knows.

**3. Is it possible to use Facebook to do a catalog party?** How many times do you have people tell you they can't have a party because they are new to the area or don't know anyone nearby? Using Facebook easily overcomes those objections. To really make this work, you need to send people to your website to look at your catalog and place orders. Many of my clients do catalog parties this way, and it works beautifully. Orders can come in from all over the country. The only thing that ships to the hostess is her hostess gift and the product she received with her hostess credit. Otherwise, these hostesses might have said, "I don't know anybody," and never have booked a party. Now, when they say, "I don't know anybody," you can say, "Do you know anybody on Facebook?"

One of the biggest benefits of using Facebook for invitations and hostess coaching is that there are fewer cancellations. You can see exactly what the hostess has done in terms of invitations; you can see how many people are attending and who they are. You know everything that is going on! It's not a mystery and you do not need to hound your hostess to take the next steps. You can actually do them for her, step in and answer people's questions and keep the excitement going.

I strongly recommend that the next time you book a party, you talk to your hostess about using Facebook for the invitations and party communications. It is highly likely to produce a successful party with much more ease and fun.

# 23: FACEBOOK® DO'S AND DON'TS

Here are a few things to pay attention to when you are using Facebook. Keep this advice in mind whenever you are posting on your wall, commenting on other's posts or responding to RSVPs and comments when you use Facebook events for hostess coaching.

**Let's start with the Do's.**

**Do be genuinely interested in others.** When somebody posts something serious—perhaps something is happening in her life that could be causing her some pain—comment on that in a very encouraging, supporting way. If somebody is excited about something, comment on that. Even if they just post, "My daughter's getting potty trained!" Comment on that.

**Do be helpful and provide useful information, bringing great energy to your conversations.** My friend, Martine Williams, shared a post about a link to a website where you can get a tool that helps you plan meals for a week, including recipes with ingredient lists. If you go to their website and you plug in your grocery store, they'll tell you what aisle those ingredients are on. For those of us who are busy, overwhelmed and exhausted, isn't that a great tip? When you come across things like that, share them on Facebook.

**Do share success stories that will help people on your team.** Perhaps it is something that you might have done at a party that got you several bookings. You can also share a story about how someone signed up. By the way, you can create a list of just your team members and post this kind of thing just to that list. You can also make it a public post or just post it to your friends, depending on how you tell the story.

**Do treat everyone with courtesy and respect.** No matter what, everyone deserves to be treated this way, and not just on Facebook!

**Do be confident.** People love to be around confident people. When you are posting on Facebook, approach your activities there from a position of confidence and high self-esteem.

**Do set time limits.** Allocate twenty minutes in the morning and twenty minutes in the evening. This is from Barbie Collins Young, who gets eighty percent of her bookings and recruits on Facebook.

**Do think before hitting that Enter button.** Have you ever posted something and then realized it was not quite appropriate? You can cancel a post or a comment that you made by using the X in the upper right of that post. However, it is a way better idea to make sure what you are posting is exactly what you want to say before you make it public.

**Do communicate only when you're competent.** This may sound obvious, but let's just state the obvious. Do not post on Facebook if you're on cold medicine, painkillers, or had a little too much wine for the evening. Wait until your head is clear and you can focus on what you are doing.

**Do take advantage of the Groups feature on Facebook.** This is a great idea if you are a leader. Consider creating a group for just your team. These are all private exchanges that the general public won't see. You might consider creating a group for hostesses, or people who love a good deal. It will make people feel special and you can do very focused, personalized communications. Do ask or inform someone before you add someone to a group, unless you are absolutely certain they belong there, like the people on your team.

### Now, let's talk about the Don'ts.

**Don't engage in religious, political, or other controversial discussions.** You'll drop friends like flies. These are topics that wherever you stand, you're passionate about it. If your friends on Facebook are on the opposite side, they're passionate too. It's best to just avoid those kinds of conversations.

**Don't post things that you wouldn't want your mom, your pastor, or your kids to see.** This may seem obvious, but you need to remember who is on your friends list and that you also want to be appropriate. Your presence on Facebook is part of your reputation, part of your brand. Keep that in mind when you are posting on Facebook.

**Don't post questionable pictures and then tag your friends who are in them.** You are not just guarding your reputation on Facebook; you need to be careful not to damage your friends' reputations as well.

**Don't ever use swear words.** Again, this is about being appropriate and about not damaging your reputation.

**Don't post anything negative about your competition.** It will not build your reputation when you tear someone else down.

**Don't spam.** As I've mentioned several times in the previous chapter, don't always be marketing on Facebook. You will turn people off and they will "unfriend" you or hide your posts.

**Don't post when you're angry.** We all say things when we're angry that we wish we wouldn't have said.

**Don't get involved in games and things like that.** Sending people kisses and hugs and poking people is just unprofessional, as is spending time playing Farmville or similar games. People will hide you or delete you. Spend your time posting interesting, useful information, great quotes and inspiring videos.

**Don't misspell.** Thank goodness for spell check! Although misspellings don't bother me, they do bother a lot of people. Check what you wrote for spelling errors before you post.

**Don't try and sell people products or services the first time you meet them on Facebook.** This is one of the biggest Don'ts. Your job is to build rapport, earn credibility and gain trust. By allowing people to get to know, like and trust you, you will develop great relationships through Facebook. Once you've established a relationship, she will ask you what you do. If it is a past acquaintance, she will ask what you are doing these days. *Then* you can talk about your product or your business opportunity.

Keep these Do's and Don'ts in mind as you spend your twenty minutes each morning and each evening on Facebook. They are basic and simple, and will go a long way to helping you make the best use of this 21st century marketing tool.

# SOME OF SHARI'S TOP-SELLING PRODUCTS INCLUDE

**The Complete Party Plan Success System Audio CD's and Success Guide**

**3 ½-hours of training includes:**

- Goal Setting
- Making An Effective Booking Call!
- Hostess Coaching That Works!
- Developing A Recruiting Mindset!
- Recruiting At Your Shows!
- Recruiting: Approach & Follow-up!
- Mock Show Presentation!
- Time Management & Organization.
- Booking Parties at Parties and Booking Parties Out & About!

**Companion Success Guide includes:**

- Sample and blank worksheets
- Sample tracking sheets
- Booking and recruiting games
- And MORE! This is a *"must have"* series.

## Off The Charts Success Audio CD's and Success Guide – 5 ½ hours of training

### 5 ½-hours of training includes:

- The Plan
- Exceptional Leadership
- The Master Key to Success
- Creating a Desire for Leadership within Your Team
- Moving Your Team into Leadership
- The 5 Keys To Effective Leadership series
- Making an Effective Booking Call
- Effective Hostess Coaching
- Recruiting at Your Parties and Effective Recruiting Approaches and Follow-Ups

### The 111-page Companion Success Guide includes:

- Getting Your Consultants Off To A Strong Start training outlines and scripts
- Tracking forms
- Sample and blank meeting outlines
- Sample and blank worksheets
- Sample scripts as well as blank templates to create your own
- Hostess coaching guide and tracking sheet
- Booking and recruiting games
- 13-step outline for coaching future and first-line leaders
- Formulas behind the plan
- Visual aids
- And much *MORE!*

## Party Tools Bundle

- 4 great products for 1 reduced price!
- 1-Pick-A-Party Theme Party binder
- 1-Dice Game (the only booking game you will ever need)
- 1-Party Cards (your fun, fast and easy 30-minute presentation)
- 1-12 Ways To Raise The Fun Meter At Your Parties audio CD

Visit www.averagetoexcellence.com to purchase any of the above products and to see a complete listing of Shari's extensive offerings.

# MORE PRAISE FOR
# SHARI HUDSPETH

"I have been using the show cards and the dice game. Well, I had a show this afternoon and I used the show cards. I love those show cards! They cover so much—from hostess benefits to the business opportunity. I had a $1,400 show with one recruit lead, one signed recruit, and five bookings! Wowza!"
—*Stacy Tennesen, Director & New Consultant Trainer, Pampered Chef*

"I had not recruited anyone since the previous summer. I purchased the Party Cards and the Dice Game, studied them and began to use both right away. I had one recruit in February, three recruits in March, one in April and one in May, with two more planning to join. I was skeptical about the Party Cards at first, but they have helped me achieve some amazing results. With the Dice Game, I am averaging at least two bookings per show! One lady joined because she said it looked so easy, she thought she could do it and even do it better than me. She was the top seller her first month in! I am on track to promote to Unit Manager in the next couple of months, and I'm also on track to win a trip to Punta Cana next year! Thank you, Shari, for your dynamic training and for all you do to help others grow great businesses."
—*Marlene Swanson, Lia Sophia*

"I did the show cards—which I love—and my hostess (who has been to many shows over the years), thought the format was easy and comfortable as well as info-packed. We played the dice game too with great results: four of the five guests played, I gave away one prize and got three bookings! WOW! The ones who booked (one was the hostess) were really excited about booking. Talk about amazing! They thought it was fun!"
—*Christa DelSorbo, Unit Leader, Creative Memories*

"There were eight people in attendance at my party. We had a lot of fun with the Party Cards and the amount of interaction. I then played the Dice Game and everyone but one guest played, including the hostess. This was one of the best parities I've done in a long time. The sales were over $800, I got five bookings, one pending, at least one fundraiser, a shower AND a potential consultant! I'm thrilled! Thank you so much for sharing these games. I can't wait to do them again!"
—*Leanne Sintniklaas, Senior Unit Leader, Epicure Selections*

"Shari's presentation at conference was much anticipated due to the fact that her Dice Game had been credited with transforming many businesses because of its ability to consistently create multiple bookings at each party! Shari took the time to tailor her presentation to reflect the language and philosophies reflective of our culture, which really helps keep the listeners focused! Shari's energy and strong delivery added even more value to the actual content. Her messages were very practical and, nearly a year later, Shari is still quoted by the leaders who heard her, which demonstrates that she left an impression upon our team. Thank you Shari!
—*Diane Nopenz - Vice President of Sales, Jockey Person to Person*

"Shari spoke at our National Conference this year and our Reps and Leaders gleaned so much from her! Specifics: Learning how to have more fun at their parties, acknowledging that we are in a crazy answering machine world, with tips on how to book parties and recruit by helping people see that they can 'take a break from the chaos'! In addition to all of that, Shari's training on booking parties through social media has been VERY well received at Wildtree and put into action immediately. We love Shari!
—*Gina Thayer, VP of Sales, Wildtree*

**To get more copies of**

**Party Plan Success!**
**From Basics to Big Results!**

**visit www.averagetoexcellence.com.**